THEY CALLED HIM BROTHER MASTERS

JOHN WESLEY MASTERS

(A MOUNTAIN PIONEER EVANGELIST)

1854 — 1924

David N. Blondell

Order this book online at www.trafford.com
or email orders@trafford.com

Most Trafford titles are also available at major online book retailers.

© Copyright 2010 David Blondell.
All rights reserved. No part of this publication may be reproduced, stored in a retrieval system, or
transmitted, in any form or by any means, electronic, mechanical, photocopying, recording, or
otherwise, without the written prior permission of the author.

Note for Librarians: A cataloguing record for this book is available from Library
and Archives Canada at www.collectionscanada.ca/amicus/index-e.html

Printed in Victoria, BC, Canada.

ISBN: 978-1-4269-2450-7 (sc)
ISBN: 978-1-4269-2451-4 (hc)

Library of Congress Control Number: 2010900170

*Our mission is to efficiently provide the world's finest, most comprehensive book publishing
service, enabling every author to experience success. To find out how to publish your book, your
way, and have it available worldwide, visit us online at www.trafford.com*

Trafford rev. 9/01/2010

Trafford www.trafford.com
PUBLISHING

North America & international
toll-free: 1 888 232 4444 (USA & Canada)
phone: 250 383 6864 ♦ fax: 812 355 4082

TABLE OF CONTENTS

PREFACE

All through my boyhood, I heard stories and anecdotes about my great grandfather, John Wesley Masters. Since his life spanned the 19th and 20th centuries, he can be described as a pioneer preacher. Since he devoted his life principally to the people in Southeastern Kentucky, he can be described as a man of the mountains. His mode of transportation was riding horseback. Grandpa Masters — the family's favorite term for him — died ten years before my birth; hence, I never knew him. The stories about him, however, lingered in the mountain communities, and the tales told by his children, grandchildren, and other family members, were legendary in nature. As a youth both the stories and the man captured my attention and imagination. Primarily, he was called J.W., sometimes, John. I will refer to him as John and J.W., and sometimes by the preferred name of the family: Grandpa Masters.

His life's work is the simple story of a self-educated, pioneer preacher/evangelist who dedicated his life to the task of the high calling of God in Christ Jesus. Not surprising, however, his story is also the story of thousands of ministers of yesterday who faced hardships, made sacrifices, experienced frequent moves in order to find work — or in Masters' case, he went where he was invited and/or challenged with preaching opportunities. He suffered hardships which in this day and time are unknown. His faith was his life. He listened for guidance and instruction from God. He was a *"Here-am-I-send-me-Lord"* kind of servant.

During my seminary days when it came time to choose a subject for my thesis, I was drawn to the only project that seemed natural for me — writing about my great grandfather. At the outset, I hoped to have enough material to meet the minimum requirement. I soon discovered I might not be equal to the task of collecting the amount of material available.

Ever since then, it has been my dream to write a biographical account of this unique mountain personality. Writing this book, therefore, is the fulfillment of a dream which started more than 45 years ago. This time I tell the story from a personal and family point of view, not in an academic setting of ibids and op-cits and references to "the writer." This time I tell it as one who has spent my ministry benefitting from the overflow of the richness and the diverseness of my great grandfather's ministry. I have come to recognize him as a man who was integrity personified.

In regard to gathering material, there were ample resources. There were his children and/or their spouses who gave information. There were other family members who reflected on memories a half century old. There were members of churches where he preached or held revival meetings (often called *protracted meetings* or simply *meetings)* in those days. Some of these folks still had vivid memories of events and sometimes details. I was allowed use of old newspaper records in Williamsburg, Corbin and London. Among other places, I spent hours and days in the Library of Lexington Theological Seminary.

All those with whom I spoke who had known him were eager to tell stories and provide bits of information. Because of the people who helped in the process, this book is a tribute to one whom they all called Brother Masters.

John Wesley Masters
1854 — 1924

ACKNOWLEDGMENTS

In 1962 I began the project of gathering material for writing this story about J.W. Masters.

I am indebted to a number of people who offered time, stories, and memories. Like him, they are now gone. My current endeavor is to take that initial writing and give it a biographical flavor in the shape and form of his life and work. I interviewed members of the family and members of congregations in Whitley, Laurel and Knox Counties in Southeastern Kentucky.

All of my interviews occurred during 1961 and 1962, while I was the minister of First Christian Church, Irvine, Ky. I have always been grateful the Irvine church not only allowed me time to pursue my seminary education, but moreover, they gave me time to travel to the various places for interviews with folks who knew John Masters.

Dr. James A. Moak, Regional Minister of the Christian Church in Kentucky at the time, gave me permission to use the Official Minutes of the Board of the Kentucky Christian Missionary Convention. The records I used were prepared by the General Secretary, H.W. Elliott., who was a contemporary of Masters. I accessed such information from the Library of Lexington Theological Seminary.

Dr. Richard M. Pope, my mentor and professor of Church History, encouraged me and gave direction and advice.

There were friends who showed interest in preserving the story of J. W. Masters. Although he has been gone for nearly a century, he still lives in the memories of various communities in the mountains of Kentucky, Virginia, and Tennessee.

Other individuals, also now gone, added to my treasury of stories and memories. With gratitude I thank them all: my father-in-law, J.B. Johnson, Sr., longtime member of First Christian Church, Williamsburg, Ky.; David Stinson of the Whetstone Christian Church in Whitley County; Joe Alsip who was a friend both from his days in Corbin as well as Lexington; my Aunt Eunice and Uncle Jasper Young, daughter and son-in-law of J.W. Masters and lifelong members of First Christian Church, Corbin, Ky.; my Uncle Shelburne Masters, son of J.W. Masters who often visited in my boyhood home; and Lila Masters, second wife of J.W. Masters.

The principle resource in writing this book was a small book by Grandpa Masters. I have no idea how many copies of the book were printed. The title is *Following the Trail of a Preacher in the Mountains of Virginia and Kentucky for Forty-seven Years*. I have often remarked that the title of this little book is almost longer than the book itself. The stories, anecdotes and other personal accounts in his book are all integral parts of his story. I felt if I did not include such material in my book, it is not likely it will be preserved anywhere else. Thus, I have liberally quoted from Grandpa's book.

Most of all, I acknowledge the encouragement, assistance, counsel and advice of my mother, Margaret LaRue Blondell. She did the initial typing of my thesis in 1962. In addition to the three copies needed for the Seminary, she also made carbons which were distributed to various descendants in the Masters family. On the night before the assignment was due, my mother sat up with me throughout the entire night editing, correcting and retyping in order for us to meet the deadline the next day. Punctuality has never been a trait in my family; but with my mom's help I delivered the thesis on time.

My mother critiqued my writing, gave suggestions for thoughts and whole segments of material, and often helped in the editing process. Without her welcomed input, my task would not have been as rich and rewarding as it was for me. Her assistance was of immeasurable value.

For a long time I have been convinced the story of John Wesley Masters is a story worth telling. I hope this writing will prove worthy in telling Grandpa Masters' story of faith, persistence, dedication and faithfulness.

INTRODUCTION

When I was in junior high school, I was handed a small, brown, paperback book to read. Although the book was regarded as a family heirloom, it was not a very old book. It just had that appearance. It took me a while, but subsequently I read the book, and characteristic of many a young boy, I soon forgot most of its contents. I was always aware, however, that Grandpa Masters had written the book. He was a pioneer, he loved the mountain people, and the book was about his evangelistic ministry among them. As much as any minister I know, he was identified with his constituents.

During high school I made the decision to enter the ministry. I began reflecting on that little book and its contents. I thought it would be interesting to read Grandpa's book again — thoroughly. My interest and desire to learn about John Wesley Masters began to build from that point on.

In conjunction with many of the anecdotal stories I often heard from members of my family, I agree that by any standard J.W. Masters was an outstanding man. He was not widely known beyond Southeastern Kentucky, and parts of Virginia and Tennessee. His training did not come in customary ways. He had no formal theological education. Had he prepared a resumé, it would have consisted primarily of love for the Lord, a sense of dedication, a willingness to do hard work, and a commitment to uphold the faith. By all measurements, inside and out, he was a large man. He stood tall. He quickly received respect from colleagues and contemporaries. Although he had this extraordinary presence and command about him, early on he had a speech impediment that would have discouraged, detracted from, and affected the role of preaching of most. Because of clergy friends who have had such challenges, I now realize and believe God uses men and women for ministry regardless of whatever physical abilities and disabilities they possess. My impression of John W. Masters is that he was, indeed, a person who stood head and shoulders above most.

In fairness, the ministry John Masters knew was totally different from what I have known as his great grandson. The problems and frustrations that defined his ministry were characterized by what most pastors in a settled ministry do not experience these days.

- He neither felt the kinds of pressures nor did he enjoy the perks of today's ministers.
- His kind of ministry did not burden him with such concerns as the recruitment of teachers for new Sunday School classes.
- He did not face working with or securing leaders for a youth program.
- He never had to respond to the incessant problems of a property committee.
- He served a church that considered nearly everything to be its mission and outreach.
- With his evangelistic style of preaching and his ministry of church establishment, he never experienced today's need for involving the membership in evangelism visitation.

The years of his ministry during the closing of the 1800s and the beginning of the 1900s presented a different set of challenges than those today. Ministerial concepts, theological environment, congregational expectations were all so much different then than they are now.

- He did not have the luxury of a seminary education.
- There were seldom easily accessible ministerial colleagues with whom he could share problems and frustrations, or dreams and desires.
- He had few resident pastorates.
- He never met with organized or functional church committees.
- While raising money was a constant concern, it is not likely that he ever dealt with raising an annual budget.
- He never lived in a parsonage. Wherever he went to speak, temporary living space was provided by friends, or he secured it on his own initiative.
- He received a meager salary as compensation for the tremendous amount of time, travel and effort he gave.
- His income was always on the low scale.
- He often went long periods without getting any pay at all.
- When he was not able to go and preach, there was little income.
- Otherwise, the only source of a stable income was determined by his part-time farming.
- He did not have an expense allowance — for lodging, food or (horse) transportation.
- There was no availability of a retirement program.
- There was no Social Security allowance.
- Health insurance was nonexistent and most expenses were always his to bear.
- He did not have the luxury of paid vacations. Time off was time down.
- He often spent long periods of time away from his wife and children.

- Continuing education and the concept of a Sabbatical for ministers were not even the figment of anyone's imagination.

This story is the story of all the ministers who have given themselves to a Cause they knew would outlive and outlast them. Brother Masters was one of a great host of pioneers whose full works and, no doubt, best achievements are known only to God.

John Wesley Masters was never a household name in the Stone-Campbell movement, which began more than two hundred years ago. Followers of Barton Stone and Alexander Campbell subscribed to a call for unity and were identified with the Restoration Movement. In the mountains of Southeastern Kentucky, Southwestern Virginia, and portions of Eastern Tennessee, however, the voice of J.W. Masters was one of a few who promoted and longed for Christian unity. Not only was he known by churches and whole communities but he was respected and loved by a like number. His memory has been dear to the hearts of these people for over a century. His work took him from mountain to mountain, valley to valley, and pulpit to pulpit.

Being a great grandson, I heard about him and his work from my father and other members of the Masters family. They told stories of the tireless efforts of this beloved ancestor. He traveled the hills of Southeastern Kentucky and Virginia for nearly 50 years. He preached thousands of sermons. He held hundreds of revivals and brought thousands of new members into the church. His only published works were a few "tracts" and the small volume already mentioned. Additionally, he organized/ started 19 congregations in those mountain communities where he preached and served. The majority of the churches had small memberships. Most of them were/are in places which are either hard to find or else non-existent today. Some of them continue to exist and are viable parts of the religious witness in their community. His record in church establishment is one that would make anyone proud, if not envious. The measure of success of a mountain evangelist was different from any other kind of public figure: sports, philanthropic, scientific, entertainment, politics.

One can learn a lot about an individual, not simply from what he says about himself and what his family says. One's reputation and esteem come from what others say. In this case, the conclusion reached is the same from both sources. In my two ministries in Southwestern Virginia and Southeastern Kentucky, I met and talked with people who knew J.W. Masters. They followed him; they listened to him preach from their pulpits; they learned from him the truths of the scriptures which he so readily quoted and by which he so faithfully lived. They entertained him in their homes with food and lodging, and at times were able to give both financial support and friendship. In return for hospitality given by these people eager to learn God's word, they were rewarded with faithful efforts and plain, simple preaching by a fellow follower of the Lord. Even though I was a couple of generations after him, I benefitted from this dedicated servant in my student appointment in Clinchport, Virginia and my first full-time pastorate in Williamsburg, Kentucky. In both regions there were people either in my church or community who had heard him preach or had known "Brother Masters."

My great grandfather and I shared a number of similar experiences. Among others, there are two principal things. Like him, early on I experienced a dilemma for those called to preach. As was he, I too was a stutterer. It began in my childhood, caused pain and embarrassment as I became a teen, and stayed with me into my college years. The proneness to stutter was always there. Even now, occasionally I find myself reflecting on some long ago event, and experience anew some of the baggage I carried from childhood into adulthood. Memories of being left out, being overlooked, being isolated are experiences that all stutterers have in common.

I was lucky. I was not subdued by the barrier those childhood and teenage problems presented. I have always attributed my *overcoming* to a concentration on the task of preaching rather than on the one doing the preaching. During my Clinchport ministry, it occurred to me one day I no longer stuttered! Fortunately through the 50 years since that time, I have remained free from the pain of those stuttering and stammering days. It is difficult for one who has never had the problem to know the injury stuttering brings.

In grade school I was not chosen for a particular event; the other kids formed a team for a spelling contest. Another time, my buddies were choosing up sides for a softball game and I was left out. I wanted to crawl under a rock. I performed in drama productions in high school, but before nearly every line I had, I would take a deep breath and try quickly to spit out the words before one of the "hang up" words *caught* me. I had trouble with words starting with "B" or "D" or "M." I virtually had to attack those words to get through them or beyond them. I began to lose some of the sting of stuttering when I took voice lessons for singing in college. Learning proper breathing control is important for stutterers. I am confident my Grandpa went through the same or similar ordeal in his youth and early adulthood. You will read of some of his reactions in his early attempts to preach. He too, was one of the lucky ones.

Another commonality I share with my great grandfather is the dream and hope for the unity of the people of God and the church of Jesus Christ. "*That they may all be one*" (John 17:21) is the dream and plea of every pioneer of the faith. The dream of the unity of God's people is a shared dream of thousands of Christians. It is another bond between my Grandpa and me.

A principle element to this story is the spirit of the times during my great grandfather's lifetime. First, it is appropriate to call those days of a century ago as "pioneering days." This implies the roughness of the wilderness, the loneliness of the trails, and the individualism of the pioneers. The pioneering spirit says essentially none of us can rely on others to do for us — we must do for ourselves. It is necessary to see those of the frontier age needed not only to be self-supporting but also self-sufficient. To be able to have information at his fingertips was perhaps the evangelist's most successful tool. Being an evangelist in my Grandpa's day required that he have quick and ready answers.

Secondly, the climate among the churches in the times of pioneer evangelists dictated a stiff spirit of competition. John W. Masters defended his faith and allowed no one (at least, without putting up a verbal fight) to speak lightly about his church. Debates were frequent and the outcome of the debates was usually determined by majority rule. In a religious debate, there was no intent for personal offense. Those engaged in arguing a point of view did not debate against opponents, but against opposing doctrines. Religious doctrines were debated as strongly from the heart (and with equal zeal) as were the issues of law on the statute books. A case in point is the historic debate between Alexander Campbell and N.L. Rice. This famous debate was held November 15-December 2, 1843, in Lexington, Kentucky. The debate focused on the "*Action, Subject, and Design of Christian Baptism.*" While the subject of such debates varied, the fervor for accuracy was always just as intent.

J.W. Masters was convinced that the church of the New Testament was the Christian Church or the Church of Christ. He used the two names interchangeably and was fully committed to the concept that his was the New Testament position and not a denominational one.

As far as possible, I have attempted to differentiate between an event and memory of that event. Family members endeavored to be as reliable as possible regarding their recollections. Some had retained documentation for such reflections.

Over the years, memory tends to fade. Remembering details that took place over a period of forty to fifty years earlier does present a challenge. Part of the reward I received in the process of the research included statements by contemporaries, his sermons notes and sermon outlines, articles about his work with churches, reading a couple of pamphlets and rereading his book. Most rewarding, however, was the personal testimony from those who knew him best. Newspaper articles or statistical reports alone cannot convey the full story of Brother Masters. Furthermore, the research provided me understanding and appreciation for the hundreds of pioneers whose ministries tell the same story as his. A greater understanding, a new appreciation for his way of life, a fuller awareness of the richness bound up in the life of the one they called Brother Masters, have all been a part of the gift I received as that reward.

Brother Masters became legend to the thousands to whom he preached. In none of the contacts I made was there anyone who could not recall pleasant memories of this mountain man. All were amazed at his ability to preach and expound the scriptures the way he did. He stood for the integrity, the simplicity, and the practicability of the scriptures. There was nothing he did, nothing he believed, nothing he preached which was not predicated upon scripture. His life was devoted to proclaiming and fulfilling the Bible. Truly, the scriptures designed his life.

At home John Masters lived a quiet, pastoral life and followed a simple lifestyle. Correspondingly, his reputation and service to the greater church did not go entirely unnoticed. During the early years of the last century, H.W. Elliott served as the Secretary to the State Board of Missions of the Kentucky Christian Missionary Convention. He held that position for more than thirty years. During the same period, Mr. Elliott held J.W. Masters in great esteem. One gets that impression from the many favorable reports he gave to the Board and the complimentary remarks made about his colleague. Furthermore, Elliott provided the following statement as an introduction in Masters' book. Hereinafter I will simply refer to his book: *Following the Trail.*

> The reading of these pages by J.W. Masters, giving us a few glimpses of his trials and victories, has been of absorbing interest to me. For the larger part of my thirty years' service as Secretary of the State Board of Missions he has enjoyed the confidence and support of that Board. This has given me an opportunity to hear from him at least once each month. He has been abundant in labors and has been always a faithful preacher of the Word and a defender of New Testament teaching. He states that he has not kept any account of the results of his labors. Many people would be glad to have a complete record of all that he has done.

In conveying the story of J.W. Masters, I am confident my feelings of admiration, respect, and honor will be quite transparent. My dream in part, is to tell a more complete story of his life and fill in between the lines as Mr. Elliott's comment suggested. My desire is to give a picture of the man, tell the stories of those whom he encountered along the trail, present some of the particulars of debates he championed, attempt to feel as he must have felt, to share in the humor he shared, and to give faces and names when possible to the statistics in the Yearbooks of the Kentucky Christian Missionary Convention. My intent is to give flesh and bone to the central character of the academic paper I wrote in 1962.

I have relied heavily upon a number of sources for telling John Masters' story. By design wherever I could, I have omitted conventional use of footnotes. Rather, I have endeavored to use footnotes to provide additional or relative information about a particular subject or matter mentioned in the story. Seemingly, footnotes which refer only to a source, date, time or place, interfere both with the flow of the story and would be contrary to the character of the one they called *Brother Masters.*

As you will see, I have used liberally many quotations: those from *Following the Trail,* the verbal quotes of the interviews, and a number of printed sources. Again, I felt including in the narrative the various references to all such sources would detract from the story itself.

In advance, I thank you for letting me tell you about my great Grandpa.

A HUMBLE BEGINNING

The Masters Family, the Dunkard Church, and the Civil War

In the mid 19th century Henry and Sallie Masters lived in Scott County, Virginia. They had five children — four boys and one girl. The oldest was John Wesley, born January 1, 1854. His three brothers and a sister were Wilson, William, Dave, and Liza. John Wesley (sometimes called John but mostly J.W.) bore the usual duties and responsibilities of being the eldest son.

Henry Masters was a farmer and a Dunkard preacher. There is little known about the branch of Christianity known as the Dunkards – a segment of the faith no longer in existence. The best known characteristic of these folks was the manner in which baptism was performed. A candidate for baptism was led into a body of water, positioned for immersion, and then "dunked" face-forward, three times (in keeping with the baptismal formula, *"in the name of the Father, Son and Holy Spirit"*). In those days times were tough, and especially for a Dunkard preacher's family. The Dunkard Church was not a mainline church, was not considered progressive, and did not attract a lot of followers. There were only certain sections of the country where a minister of this church could live and provide for a family of any size. Especially was this true for the size of Henry and Sallie Masters' family.

The years seemed to pass rather swiftly, however, with little information available about much of J.W.'s boyhood. With vivid memories he was later able to recall for his children tales about the cold winters he and his brothers experienced in attending school as young boys. His daughter Eunice Young said when it was cold weather the boys would take turns and push each other to school in a wheelbarrow. Even when it was freezing, they did not always have shoes. When there were no shoes they went to school barefoot, taking turns riding and pushing each other in the wheelbarrow. While one boy pushed (the garden cart), his brothers were able to secure a measure of relief from the frozen ground and the biting wind by rubbing and warming their feet with their hands as they rode along. They each took turns in the practice of teamwork.

The Civil War and the period of the 1860s focused on the controversy between the North and the South. Henry Masters found himself in a dilemma. Being opposed to slavery he was a Union sympathizer. The decision either to join the Confederate Army like his neighbors or leave his home state of Virginia was not easy. He worried that his family would not be cared for if he were gone. He was concerned for his wife and small children and what would happen to them. Henry Masters tried time and time again to avoid the Confederate soldiers. Mrs. Lila Masters (second wife of J.W. Masters) supplied an early boyhood experience of her late husband related to the war. She always referred to him as "Mr. Masters."

> Mr. Masters said that when they lived in Scott County, Virginia, many were the times his father would hide in the fodder-shocks and anywhere else he could. He said the Rebels would come after his father. On one occasion, when he had hidden in a fodder-shock, his father decided he ought to move, and for some strange reason he did. He went up into the woods and hid. He had not been there long when the Rebels came and tore the fodder-shocks all to pieces, in their unsuccessful attempt to find him.

A similar story about those Civil War days comes from Mrs. B.C. Johnson, a niece of J.W. Masters.

> In order to protect his family, one night his father (Henry Masters) lay outside all night and covered himself with a blanket. During the night it snowed and the next morning the tracks of the Rebel soldiers were all around him, but they hadn't touched him. He evidently had been asleep and didn't know how very near the soldiers had been.

> On another night the soldiers of the Confederacy came and knocked at the door and Grandma (J.W.'s mother) said, "Now, do not come in here — the children are afraid of you." The children were all there, it happened when Uncle John was little. Grandpa was right there on the backside of the bed, lying behind the children next to the wall. The top layer was a featherbed and underneath was a straw bed. The bed was pushed next to the wall. He pressed the straw down and the featherbed was right over him, and no one could tell the difference. Grandma begged them not to come in. They told her to open the door or they would knock it down. She didn't open it, she just laid still. They came in and looked everywhere. She lay there in the bed with the children and she told the soldiers that he wasn't there. Grandpa had gone that day and bought two or three of the boys a pair of boots, and as the soldiers started out the door they picked up all the children's boots and took them out to the forks of the road and left them. Sallie Masters said because of his fright, her husband was so close to her, she could hear his heart beating from where she was in the bed.

Finally Henry Masters, Dunkard preacher, opposed not only to slavery but also to fighting, could put it off no longer. He knew he had to leave Virginia. He moved to Magoffin County, Kentucky. We do not know whether or not his move included the role of Pastor of a church in Kentucky. We do not know if he had friends or even family in the new community. Whatever was his pull to this remote section of the state, he moved his young family to this Kentucky mountain community. The move came approximately at the time J.W. was ten years old. He later wrote in his book that their family lived there for ten years, returning to Virginia in 1874. From 1864 until 1874 the Henry Masters family lived in Magoffin County, probably in the community which is now known as Salyersville, Kentucky. If this is correct, during his preaching days, when he visited in this community to hold revival meetings, J.W. was returning to the people among whom he had spent a good portion of his childhood.

A Young John W. Masters

Jobs and Careers

As early as age 10, J.W. was beginning to formulate thoughts about ministry. Like any young boy, he looked up to his father with admiration. He was influenced by his father and he wanted to be like him. Since Henry Masters was a Dunkard preacher, J.W. told him when he grew up he wanted to be a Dunkard preacher just like him. Contrary to how most Dunkard preachers dressed, however, the elder Masters wore a tie and kept his hair cut short. Dress code had nothing to do with young John's interest in the ministry. From early on, J.W. had a keen interest in the Bible. The actual time between expressing interest in ministry and making a formal decision, followed a period of years and the consideration of other work endeavors. One such possibility was to be a lawyer. This possibility was suggested to him by his employer, Mr. E.R. Conley. He was an industrious young boy and at the time worked as a hired hand at a salary of ten cents per day while still living in the Salyersville community. Often, he remembered, his work equaled that of the men on the same job who were being paid five times the amount he received. He noted the inequity of work expectation for him at one salary level and others at another. Nonetheless, he remained with the job.

J.W. worked for nearly five years for Mr. Conley. No doubt the work of the lad pleased Conley, or Conley would not have kept him for that long a period of time. Another indicator that they enjoyed a friendship was the influence Mr. Conley had on his young hired hand in suggesting he should study to be a lawyer. W.W. Howes, Conley's uncle, was a lawyer and invited the young John Masters to go home with him, stay with him and study hard, and he would make him a lawyer and not charge him for his training. Conley encouraged the young Masters to go, and even offered to furnish his clothing. Even though J.W. agreed to these proposals, the thought of being a preacher still persisted in his eager mind. His statement from his book says what he thought.

I gladly accepted the offer, and decided to go and make a lawyer of myself. "But I must go to school a year before I begin the study of law," was my thought. And before the year ended I decided that I could not make a successful lawyer and a preacher both. "And by the help of the Lord," I said, "I will try to make a preacher and let other men make lawyers of themselves."

His compelling interest in the church came during his teen years. He devoted a lot of time to Bible study. He tells how he decided what he would do regarding the many voices of the church speaking to him. Among these, he was looking and listening for the voice of the Dunkard Church, but failed to find the name in the Bible.

I went to my father, Bible in hand, and asked him to turn down a leaf where I could read about the Dunkard Church. And to my surprise, he said: "It is not in the Bible." My thought was is it possible that father belongs to a church that the Bible says nothing about? I told him that I had aimed to join the Dunkard Church, but, if it is not in the Bible, I will never join it. "Are you going to join the Baptist Church, Methodist or the Presbyterian?" he asked. I said: "Are they in the Bible?" "No, none of the denominations are in the Bible." "Well, Father, I have read of a church in the Bible, what one is it?" "Oh, that is the church of Christ." He replied, "That is the only one for me." It was not long after this until father quit being a Dunkard and was satisfied with being a Christian only. My father later baptized me.

Young Masters attended school in communities in addition to Magoffin County. He also attended school in Virginia and Tennessee. Whatever sort of education he received is hard to know. Mrs. Lila Masters remembered, "In those days there were schools held in log houses, and the only sort that resembled the public school of our day was their 'three-months' school." Their terms were short, held in the fall of the year and ended about Christmas. Like all of the other children of his day, she said Masters probably used the old Blue-Back speller and the McGuffey Reader. Following the family's return to Virginia, J.W. attended school in his home community and also in Tennessee. His home in Scott County was not far from the Tennessee line and apparently he attended school either in Kingsport or Bristol; both communities are in Sullivan County.

An Interest in A Good Education

After finishing his education in the Virginia public school system, since a teaching certificate was not a requirement, J.W. taught school for awhile. Whether his teaching was comparable to that of other schoolmasters in those days is not known. Taking a cue from the experience regarding his intentions to become a lawyer, we know the standards and requirements for being a teacher likewise were different from what they are today. Masters mentioned in his book that his first school was in Virginia. My great Aunt Eunice said that was in Fairview, Virginia. We do not know if this was his first role as a teacher. Based on my great grandfather's later pattern of making rather frequent moves from one place to another, it would be safe to surmise that during those years he taught in other schools too. That observation is made simply on the fact that Fairview is quite a distance from Scott County where the family lived. It stands to reason his teaching was in either the three-months school or six-months school. The six-month school was a later development than the earlier pattern.

It was during the time he was teaching in his first school, not far from his birthplace, that Masters continued to focus on Bible study. Moreover, somewhat as companion reading he was also studying sermons by Ben Franklin.[1] He had a desire to preach and uphold the gospel to the best of his ability. This interest had

---

[1] In a small, three-volume set of sermons, entitled New Testament Christianity, edited by Z. T. Sweeney, Cincinnati, Standard Publishing Co., 1929, there are preserved several of Ben Franklin's sermons. Although I have no knowledge of the book of sermons mentioned above, some of the books of sermons Masters read (and possibly used in his preaching) may be in the following: The Kingdom of God; Positive Divine Law; Inauguration of the New Institution; New Testament Example of Conversion; The Course to Pursue to Be Infallibly Safe; Conversion, or Turning to God; and How Are Persons Made Believers? Surely, sermons like these would make good material for the young preacher starting out with no other knowledge of how to preach. Evidence of his preaching tells us he followed this style.

become known throughout the community. Understandably during his early days he was not the able, strong opponent in defending his beliefs about the Bible, or his position on the Restoration Plea as he most ably proved later. Nonetheless, it was in this first teaching experience that he was challenged to his first debate.[2]

He was challenged by a Methodist preacher; and readily accepted. After the debate Masters was very confident, enough so that he described the outcome as "victory was won for the truth." He failed to record the subject of the debate, but he obviously felt his side was the side of the truth. The debate was likely held in Sloan's schoolhouse, where he later preached. When he first became bothered by a stuttering problem is not clear. However much his stuttering bothered him, it was not enough to deter him from his love for ministry and his desire to preach.

In addition to his respect and admiration for his father's ministry, this determination to become a minister and preach was possibly due in part to the influence of a preacher in Virginia by the name of John Carter. Due to later comments, Carter's influence may have been stronger than that of his own father. While it cannot be substantiated, family members thought John Carter helped persuade young John Masters to come into the Christian faith. Even though his father, Henry Masters, baptized him, it is likely through the leading of the Reverend Mr. John Carter, that young John Masters committed himself to ministry and to the pursuit of a lifelong dream: the desire to preach the Gospel.

---

[2]   Although this was his first debate, there is no record and no way of knowing how many debates J.W. Masters had in his lifetime. His ministry extended almost half a century, and, according to his own statement, he had a debate before he ever preached his first sermon. In an interview with Masters' son, Shelburne H. Masters, (himself a minister) Uncle Shelly (as we often called him) told me that his father loved to defend his faith in debates. He never asked for nor sought debates, but always accepted when challenged. Uncle Shelly not only followed his father into the ministry of preaching, but also into the art of debating. Uncle Shelburne told me in more than forty-four years of ministry, he held thirty-two debates. No doubt, in fifty years, his father at least equaled or perhaps doubled that record.

David N. Blondell

Making up his mind to be a minister was difficult. A factor of primary importance to any would-be preacher is the ability to speak publicly. By this time J.W. Masters had grown to be a very good-sized man, over six feet tall. For many years his bigness of soul and heart and his desire to preach the Gospel were juxtaposed by the smallness of his ability to make a speech. During his first years of preaching in churches and in his attempts at speaking to audiences in public debate, it was apparent he had a long way to go before accomplishing his dream of winning people to Jesus Christ. No definition would have classified him as an orator or public speaker.

Facing Up to Stuttering

J.W. quickly acknowledged and faced up to his shortcomings in public speaking. He had been handicapped by his stuttering since childhood, and now it was weighing most heavily on his mind and a real source of concern. Most likely family and friends had pointed out to him his lack of a gift of fluent speech. Parenthetically, I well remember when I made public my decision to go to school to become a preacher, one dear lady in my home church took it upon herself to counsel me. She was well aware of my stuttering. Her advice for me was to go to school and get into some aspect of ministry — she mentioned Christian Education or Youth ministry or church music — something other than the pulpit ministry. I felt keenly her interest in wanting to protect me from the embarrassment of relying principally on public speaking to fulfill my desire to be a minister. I was not even out of high school when I made that decision. My only model for ministry had been that of a preacher. In my home church there was no minister of Christian Education, no minister of Youth, no paid music ministry. To me ministry was preaching. I am confident my great grandfather felt the same and would have inwardly appreciated but completely rejected such sage advice as not putting himself through the pain and agony of attempting to be a preacher. I made the same choice he did.

It seemed the more intense concentration he gave to the problem, the greater stress it caused him. There was no time when he was not conscious of his dilemma. Anticipating a career which would require him to do public speaking seemed certain to bring him failure and disappointment. Advice for ways to overcome his stammering came from different sources. His first sermon was done at the school house as he tried to implement such advice.

> One Mr. Scott had told my mother to have me
> carry a bullet in my mouth — that it would help me
> to overcome the habit. You see, I went to Stone's

prepared, with the bullet in my pocket. [He had been invited to preach at the home of Mr. Henry Stone.] Just before getting up from my chair I put the bullet in my mouth. I read my text from Ephesians 2:10. I suppose I had been talking for fifteen minutes, when I choked with embarrassment and swallowed the bullet. I tried to cough it up, as it was the only one I had with me. I was not alarmed in the least at swallowing it, for I guess I had swallowed a pint of hog-rifle bullets before.

In a few weeks I tried my luck the second time, but, to be sure not to swallow the bullet, I cut it half-way and put a string in it and mashed it together and tied a knot in the other end of the string and held it between my teeth, so you see there was no swallowing that bullet. While trying to deliver the second sermon the bullet dropped out of my mouth, dangling about my chin. The people laughed. I — well, you can guess what I did then. I sat down.

Before making the third effort, I went to the woods up on a mountainside and preached to the trees and rocks. I did not stutter this time. I went to Sloan's Schoolhouse and tried again. After I had preached and dismissed the crowd, a Baptist preacher who was present and had refused to adjourn the audience, began answering my sermon. After he closed I was replying, and a Methodist friend jumped up in my face, saying: "I will go to hell before I will be baptized." I said: "Go on, I would not care if you were there now." I was excited, mad and foolish, you know. After I had time to get my wits together, I asked God to forgive me, and I would have asked the man's pardon could I have seen him again.

During those early years of Masters' attempts at preaching, Professor Joseph Hopwood, President of Milligan College, Tennessee, heard the young Masters preach one night. Going home after the service that night, Masters was walking behind a group and heard this comment by professor Hopwood, "Well, if that boy ever makes a preacher, he'll fool me." That was the beginning of a beautiful friendship. On many occasions thereafter, President Hopwood singled out Masters in order to give him both advice and counsel. The friendship between these two grew and they enjoyed the companionship of one another many times. President Hopwood made it known that he was very fond of J.W. Masters.

Gaining experience and expertise at the task of preaching came hard for this novice minister. After he had been preaching about three years, Masters was told that a church which had obviously heard him preach, had appointed a committee to talk with him about giving up preaching. They determined that because his attempts at public speaking were so feeble, he should quit. The good brother who conveyed this message to Masters asked the committee to wait awhile and give him another chance. Needless to say, after this, he was more determined than ever to improve in his speaking and preaching and did everything he could think of to become better. It was only after he had been successful enough to baptize his three brothers and his only sister that he felt the committee would not make their visit to him in order to persuade him to give up preaching.

A Return to His Roots

In 1878, Masters was 24 years old and by this time had returned to his birthplace in Scott County, Virginia. It isn't known exactly how long he had been there, or how he came to know her, but he had been there long enough to meet, court, and subsequently propose marriage to Rebecca Ann Robinett. Their wedding followed soon thereafter. Rebecca was born on February 14, 1856, and the daughter of Sampson Robinett and Mary Ann Meal Robinett. Rebecca was two years younger than J.W.

A little more than a year following their marriage, their first child, Orville Jack, was born on September 2, 1879, to these young parents. About a year and a half passed before the birth of their second child, Sallie Irene Masters, on March 17, 1881. Within another year and a half their second daughter, Annie Sue, arrived. No birth date is recorded for her. Soon, however, tragedy struck their happy home. With little or no warning, the joy J.W. and Rebecca experienced regarding the birth of their new infant daughter, quickly turned into mourning. Annie Sue died on August 2, 1882.

During this period of time Masters was attempting to both farm and preach. Truth be told, he did not seem to be making progress with either. With the responsibilities of a growing family, he determined that he had to do one or the other, but could no longer attempt to do both. Because his heart remained fixed on preaching, he gave up farming except as a hobby.

Sometimes because of and sometimes in spite of his preaching, the reputation of this young man was beginning to spread. For a time, he made his home in Fairview, Virginia, where he taught school. Most likely, it was in Fairview when his next opportunity came to defend his religious convictions in a debate. A local Baptist preacher was challenging the Campbellites for a debate, and J.W. Masters was invited to come and debate with him.

In a 1939 publication, *Sketches of Our Mountain Pioneers*, John W. West commented about this debate in Fairview which took place in the closing years of the 19th century. It became well known that my great grandfather detested the nickname Campbellite. Since there seemed to be no one else to stand up against this slur, J.W. Masters took on the task. The following account is by J.W. West.

Brother Masters entered the place of worship and the preacher was singing "like a lark" and was apparently in the best of health. Brother Masters approached him in the pulpit and introduced himself and informed him that he was there to accept his challenge for a debate. He then read a proposition which included the following:

- First, Baptist name;
- Second, Baptist vote on the fitness of candidates for membership;
- Third, closed communion;
- Fourth, mourner's bench system (Southern Baptists in the mountains used the mourner's bench at the time);
- Fifth, Final perseverance − the claim that one cannot fall from grace;
- Sixth, Repentance before faith.

Brother Masters then said to him, "You show me these in the Bible and I will let you vote me into the Baptist church tonight." The preacher replied, "I am sick, too sick to speak tonight." Brother Masters said, "Show me one of them and I will take the balance." The preacher again replied, "I am sick." Brother Masters replied, "Get better by morning and we will try it."

Several Baptists near the pulpit overheard the conversation and doubted very much that their preacher was sick, judging from the way he had been singing when Brother Masters entered.

The next morning when the people gathered, their preacher was not present. All concluded that he was not sick either, except as Brother Masters had made him psychologically sick. Seeing that he had shown he was unwilling to face his challenger, one of his own followers said, "I believe our pastor knows he is wrong, and I for one bid him good-bye."

About that time another person said, "I am with you." And then a third said, "The same dog bites me." This is both an example of mountain language and a sense of mountain honesty that folks expressed when they were convinced of something. Brother Masters was thus able to organize a Church of Christ there and secure a minister for them.[3]

Due to this sort of circumstance, J. W. Masters began to receive many invitations to preach and uphold his religious convictions. For example, Masters recorded the following account about a union meeting at a "church-house," held by a Baptist preacher from Kentucky and a Methodist preacher from Lee County, Virginia.

They were having a red-hot revival. The Baptist preacher sent for me to come down, and said he wanted to preach a sermon for me. I went that night. As I entered the door some one pointed me out to the preacher. He arose and read Acts 8:26: *"See, here is water. What hinders me to be baptized?"*

The preacher said: "This question was asked eighteen hundred years ago, and one of you could ask me the same one tonight." Then for more than an hour he skinned and salted "Campbellites."

---

[3]   Let it be noted: the list of congregations in Appendix C, established by Masters, does not include this one in Fairview.

Finally, being exhausted, he quit and called on the old Methodist brother to conclude, who said: "Enough has been said, such as it is." The Baptist said: "Be here tomorrow at the regular hour. Let us be adjourned."

At that moment I arose and asked permission to speak; he granted it and sat down. I began by saying: "I have been a hired boy all or most of my life, and when I did a day's work, a month's work or a job for a man I was anxious to know what he thought of it. Your preacher sent for me to come down; that he wanted to do a job for me, and I suppose he wants to know what I think of it, and he will soon learn. He said the question of his text was asked eighteen hundred years ago; that is true. He said, again, that one of you could ask him the same question to-night. That is also true. Now, what I want to know is, would he give you the same answer that the God-sent preacher gave eighteen hundred years ago?" Just then he came to his feet, saying: "This is my congregation and I will adjourn it; stand and be dismissed." So the crowd was dismissed.

I said: "All who want to hear me, sit down." He said: "Let's all go." An old Methodist man, who grew up with my father and mother and seemed to think as much of me as he did his son, was sitting at the door and said to the preacher: "You have got to hear Masters. You thought you were doing something great hackling on what you call 'Campbellites,' and you think that Masters has no friends here because he has no brethren here. I want you to know that he has as many friends here as you have, and I am one of them." The preacher, in the meantime, was getting ready to go. The man at the door said: "Now, I will tell you that I will tear every rag from your back before I will let you out." Some of his brethren spoke, saying: "Sit down."

He sat down, then the man at the door said: "Brother Masters, get in that pulpit, and if you can't skin that preacher without skinning us Methodists, just skin us, for God knows that I am willing to be skinned just to see him skinned." I talked about thirty minutes and said to the preacher: "If you are not satisfied with this, I will meet you here tomorrow." Tomorrow came and a large crowd on hand, but as the newly elected constable said when asked by the court where a certain witness was, "He is omnipresent" — that meant he was not there. This was an end to the union revival meeting at Fairview, Virginia.

Security and Medicine

While Masters' reputation as a preacher was growing, opportunities to give his growing family financial support were not. Thus, as before he faced the problem of future support for his family. He was certainly not getting rich from his preaching. In point of fact, making ends meet was a constant concern. Giving up preaching, however, was the last thing in the world this freshman preacher wanted to do.

Dr. Silas E. Shelburne was a dear friend. Unaware or not about his rather recent exploits in the study of medicine, Dr. Shelburne told J.W. he wanted him to come and live near his home and study medicine. This time the proposal was a little sweeter. Masters remarked about this proposal, "He would put me into practice free of charge, and I could support my family by practicing medicine and preaching at the same time." He decided to accept the proposition to study medicine. At the same time he received a proposal from L.C. Shelburne, a brother to the doctor. Living nearby, Mr. Shelburne was aware of Masters' financial difficulties and offered a house for him and his family. It goes without saying that the young father was eager to make his way in the world — accommodating both his love for his family and his love for preaching. He thought this was almost too good to be true. Nonetheless, it also seemed to be the right thing to do. The initiator of this whole matter was Dr. Shelburne, whom Masters held in high regard. Later Masters wrote that he considered Dr. Shelburne to be "a hero among the disciples of the Old Dominion."

Common knowledge tells us that the standards for the practice of law, as mentioned earlier, the practice of medicine, and the qualifications for teaching were very different then than they are today. It seems no profession has been exempt from continuing to stiffen requirements for each discipline as they have changed through the late 19th century, into the 20th and now into the 21st century.

The opportunity to acquire a formal education, then as now, gave one an advantage. In most professions it would have been a prerequisite. During the lifetime of this young preacher, there was more emphasis placed upon firsthand experience than upon classroom knowledge. In regard to the field of medicine, a study of the bones of the body was primary. Therefore, with the use of medical books and a skeleton for his personal educational ventures, one more time J.W. Masters was willing to pursue yet another choice in a career. He used an upstairs room in his new home for a study. He wrote about this venture, "I read and studied hard for some ten mouths or more. All the while I felt uneasy, fearing that I was not doing the wise thing."

Although he wanted security for his family, he still had that lingering and haunting question of personal satisfaction in his heart and soul. There seemed to be the kind of inner calling that must have come to Abraham of old when it drew him away from all family and friendly ties. Abraham felt and heard an alluring call that bid him go into a land where he had the assurance of nothing or no one, except God. There is no doubt, J.W. Masters fought the battle of that same inner struggle. Nothing he tried which took him away from the field of evangelism seemed to satisfy him. There was no area of business with which he felt comfortable. There was nothing about the practice of law which fulfilled him. Neither was there contentment in the pursuit of medicine. Teaching provided him only so much satisfaction. He could not justify the end by the means. This awareness within him finally was brought out one day when he observed a minister passing by on his way to a meeting. (*Meeting* was the popular term for revival.) He heard Brother White singing, "The heaven bells are ringing, and I am going home." Masters' book contains this snapshot of his struggle.

> I felt that I must go, but here I am tied up. My eyes filled with tears. My heart swelled with grief. I fell on my knees and said: "O God, my Father, sink or swim, live or die, I am going to preach." I arose to my feet, put the books in one sack and the skeleton in another, carried them over to the

doctor, and said, "Here, Doctor, are your books and bones." He said. "Well, what do you mean?" I answered, "I mean to preach," and I was expecting a scolding, but (God bless the Doctor!) he looked at me earnestly for a moment and said: "Go on, and so long as I have a dollar you shall not suffer." And he made that promise good.

After that, both Shelburne brothers gave a great deal of financial help to the young preacher and his family. Through the years the brothers remained very dear and close to J.W. Masters.

A Unique Financial Proposal

Masters' father-in-law, Sampson Robinett, was a strong member of the Baptist Church. From time to time he tried to persuade J.W. to join his church. J.W. said Robinett offered him bribes in order to get him to become a Baptist. Robinett was fairly wealthy and he knew his son-in-law was "poor, and getting poorer day by day, because the Christian Churches in that section of Virginia hadn't yet been taught their duty about supporting the ministry." (Whatever truth there was to such a statement by Masters, it is true the Baptist church is known for emphasis upon stewardship and giving financial support for the ministry and mission of the church.)

In 1884 J.W. and Rebecca and their family lived on the Robinett farm belonging to Masters' father-in-law, Sampson Robinett. One day at the close of the service of a Baptist meeting, one of the members of the church (who evidently had been sent by the elder Robinett) spoke to J.W., telling him he wanted to go home with him for dinner. After their Sunday dinner, the visitor invited Masters to take a walk with him around the farm. He suggested J.W. take a good look at it. During the course of their round, the self-invited guest asked his host how much money the farm was worth. Masters told his guest he had no idea. At that point, the gentleman told Masters he was authorized to tell him the farm would be his if he would just make one little jump. When Masters asked just what kind of jump, the man said it was a jump "into the Baptist Church." Hearing that, the proud, young minister promptly replied, "You go back and tell the old boss that I would not leave the church of Jesus Christ, and stay all night with the Baptist Church, for all that he is worth." End of subject. End of conversation. End of debate about joining the Baptist Church. The issue never surfaced again.

Although they were together many times after that, Masters and his father-in-law never could see eye to eye on religious matters. Due to his inability to out-evangelize the young evangelist, Sampson Robinett left no inheritance to his daughter and son-in-law. He left each of his sons $20,000. A like amount of money, however, was not enough to influence J.W. Masters to relinquish his religious convictions. The value and rewards of his faith were calculated differently than that measured in monetary terms. In withholding an equal portion of his estate from his daughter and her family, Mr. Robinett may have fulfilled the letter of the tithing/giving law, but he totally missed the spirit of that principle.

This attempted bribe came at a very inopportune time for this young minister. Although he held fast to his faith, J.W. could not shake the haunting feeling of wishing he could provide better living conditions for his family. Shortly after this, my great grandfather concluded that he could not continue to do the same thing he had been doing and expect different results. He further concluded he needed to change his routine if he wanted different results in achieving a better financial base for his family. Because of the wishy-washiness of this dilemma, and apparently desperate for some means of additional income, one more time he was enticed with the thought of becoming a lawyer. Judge Richmond was an acquaintance, and J.W. counseled with him about securing admittance to the bar. He quickly learned such a hope was not possible. There was no shortcut to the process. The Judge encouraged J.W. to begin studying law. Even though this would mean giving up his pursuit of ministry, he agreed to consider the matter further. Before changing the direction of a career yet again, he reasoned he could not succeed both as a lawyer and as a preacher. Battling within himself, his struggle again proved overwhelming and his first love won out. So overpowering was his desire to preach the Gospel — and promote the Restoration Plea — this time he abandoned forever the idea of becoming a lawyer.

An Old Nemesis

In the early part of 1885[4] Masters went to the "corner house in Washington County Virginia to hold a meeting." At this pivotal juncture in his life, it was called to his attention rather painfully that he faced an old nemesis. He still had not mastered his most necessary tool — a command of speech. What he had to say was apparently being all but wasted on some folks due to his inability to say it succinctly and clearly. Every successful preacher or evangelist knows one speaks to draw attention to the message, not messenger. Grandpa Masters once wrote a track about speaking in tongues. He quoted scripture from the Day of Pentecost in the book of Acts regarding the necessity for plain and understandable language. No one more than he, knew of the importance of clarity and distinctiveness in conveying the Gospel. He knew he must improve his speaking ability.

Walking to his lodging place after the first night's service and thinking that he had done a very decent job with his sermon, he approached several people in front of him who were unaware of his presence. He simply slackened his pace and walked along behind. Of all things, they were discussing his preaching. His own words:

> One man said, "That was the poorest effort I ever heard from the pulpit." Another one said, "Poor fellow! I am sorry for him. His friends need to have him quit trying to preach." That was all I wanted to hear. I waited for them to go on out of my hearing. Behind me came another crowd. They were also talking about the preacher. I slowed my gait to hear what was being said. One said: "Poor boy, if he ever makes a preacher, it will

---

4   There is no way to determine the precise year of the incident referred to in this narrative. But according to an incident just following this account, we can be reasonably sure that we are in the ballpark of the appropriate time period.

be in another world and not in this." That night I rolled and tumbled from one side of the bed to the other. I prayed to the Lord and asked Him to help me take courage and keep on trying.

Seemingly, his prayers had a rather immediate answer, for he remained there two weeks and had a successful revival. According to some records, he was even called back later to conduct a second revival at the same Washington location.

Another Old Nemesis

The nature of evangelistic preaching meant that evangelists were without a regular place to conduct the preaching; hence, there was another old nemesis. Masters still faced the old financial predicament which constantly plagued him and his family. It was as if he would take one step forward, and then two back. The money problem lingered. There was no regular income. If he could just manage for awhile longer, he knew spring was approaching and good weather would bring opportune traveling time. His wife Rebecca was expecting another child within a few months and he did not want her to face this new trial with continued financial uncertainty. With no more assurance or more permanent financial security than just hoping from day to day, it was inevitable something had to change.

That spring, in the latter part of May, 1885, J.W. Masters and his father-in-law embarked on a trip westward. As sometimes is the case, one or more sons-in-law often call their father-in-law "Boss." [Parenthetically, I had such a family in my last pastorate. I am not sure of the precise origin of the term, nonetheless, I was always aware of the respect his sons-in-law had for this saintly gentleman.] J.W. and his father-in-law had a similar relationship. He often made reference to Mr. Robinett as "Boss." Mr. Robinett wanted to go to Missouri but Masters had a desire to go to Lexington, Kentucky. Each one of them owned a horse. They hitched the horses to a buggy and drove into Cumberland Gap, Tennessee. There they left their horses and traveled by train into the adjoining state, Kentucky.

Nearing Cumberland Gap, Masters wished to stop to see who now lived in a house formerly occupied by a friend. Using the subtle humor he acquired early, the story he tells served to cushion difficult situations for him throughout his entire life.

I went to the door, and there sat an aged couple.
I asked them where Mr. Eads had gone. The old
woman said: "He moved West." "What church did

he belong to?" I asked. [With his sense of humor well documented, I can imagine he asked this question purely for the sake of amusement.] "The Campbellite Church," she said. I asked her if there were Campbellites in that section. "A few," she said. I said, "Good woman, I have been hearing of those people, but never saw any of them. I would like to hear one preach." "I would not go ten steps to hear one preach," she replied. "Why, what kind of people are they?" I asked. "They do not believe in heartfelt religion, nor anything that is good," was her answer. I said, "Well, they have no sense, have they?" She said, "Mister, their preachers are mighty smart." The Boss, sitting out there in the buggy and hearing it all, was so tickled that he just laughed so hard that you could have heard him a hundred yards. Of course, you imagine my smile. The old man saw my smile and said, "Old woman, you might say too much; that man might be one himself." "Are you, Mister?" said the old lady. I said, "No, but people of low breed call me one." She said: "Now, I never heard one preach, but that is what they say about them."

That was the type of humor J.W. Masters enjoyed. Although he could joke about being a Campbellite, as I remarked earlier, he did not like the name nor did he ever refer to himself as such. When I was young, I remember hearing family members often quote Grandpa Masters in using the phrase which he did with the old woman in Cumberland Gap. The incident above simply underscores its validity.

It is not clear just why Masters wanted to go to Lexington. There is little question it was merely for enjoyment, times were too hard for such a trip. It is probable it had to do with the pursuit of a better income and financial stability. It is also likely that through a contact in his work in Virginia he had heard preachers were needed in Kentucky. For whatever reason, they arrived in Lexington in due time. While they were there they stayed in the home of Mr. Robinett's brother-in-law, approximately four miles outside town in a community where there was a church called Republican Church.[5] The people in the community learned of the visitors from Virginia and a man contacted them and arranged for Brother Masters to conduct a revival the following September.

Not long after returning to his home in Fairview, Virginia, Rebecca presented her husband with his second son. David Garfield Masters was born August 1, 1885.

---

[5] There is a congregation in Lexington called South Elkhorn Christian Church. At one time its name was Republican Christian Church, but years ago the name was changed to South Elkhorn Christian Church. Church historian Dr. Richard M. Pope, served as Chair of the Board, and told me about the name change.

A Turning Point

Young Garfield Masters was little more than a month old when his father left home on a mission which was destined to alter the life of the growing Masters family. Masters could not know that early fall morning when he left the mountains of Virginia that this missionary journey would be of more significance than its many predecessors. He had no idea it would mark the needed turning point in either his personal affairs or his professional career. He could not know the time was near when, in a totally new field, he would reap a bountiful harvest in his labors for his Master.

John W. Masters returned to Lexington to fulfill his engagement at the Republican Christian Church. As he traveled by horseback, he arrived in Barbourville, Kentucky. He remained there for several days, preaching each night. During that brief stay, folks in the community talked about having him preach regularly once a month. Some congregations had full-time pastors. Dozens of small churches joining the Stone-Campbell Restoration Movement all across Kentucky were unable to afford the luxury of full-time preaching. He left Barbourville and continued his journey by horseback to London. From London he traveled by train to Lexington. He fulfilled the commitment made earlier to conduct a revival for the Republican Church in Fayette County, Kentucky.

It was on this visit to Lexington that John W. Masters met J.W. McGarvey, President of the Kentucky State Board of Missions, whose successor is The Christian Church in Kentucky, and is affiliated with the Christian Church (Disciples of Christ). Out of this meeting a lasting friendship grew and developed between the two men. Masters was informed by McGarvey that the State Board was interested in securing someone to preach in the region of Barbourville. Masters immediately acknowledged his interest in the assignment of being the minister of this Knox County congregation.

On his return trip homeward, he again visited Barbourville and learned of the visit by the Secretary of the State Board. In his visit, J.B. Jones' promised support from the Board for one-fourth time. The church would make the choice of who would preach for them. The offer was made and the offer was subsequently accepted.

For the first time in his on-again off-again efforts at full time ministry, John W. Masters had reached the next level of ministry. He was about to experience what it was like to be the regular minister/pastor of a congregation.

Growing A Ministry

Days in Barbourville and Knox County

Beginning a new ministry in Kentucky by no means necessitated cutting off ties in Virginia. In years to come, he returned to his home state a number of times to hold evangelistic meetings. Sometimes that even meant establishing churches. Making the transition from his former residence to the new one was not as easy as he had presumed. During the first three years in Kentucky, he also maintained his residence in Virginia. He rode horseback once each mouth from Fairview to Barbourville, a distance of eighty-five miles. He made these monthly trips to his new pastorate for three years.[6] During this time he missed only one month due to high water that made the trail impassable.

During his early ministry in Barbourville Masters conducted three revivals in churches in the nearby area. He established congregations in Artemus and Trosper — both small communities in Knox County, Ky. In a conversation I had with my uncle Shelburne Masters, he said he was not sure whether or not his

---

6 Perhaps it would be appropriate to say that I have never read anything or heard anyone make reference to J.W. Masters being ordained. Through his own writing there were frequent incidences when he spoke about becoming or making a minister of himself, but never any reference to being ordained to the ministry. There is no doubt that such an occurrence took place. It was never mentioned. There is nothing in print relating to his ordination or his being called "Reverend" until the time of his pastorate in Corbin, Ky., in the early 1890s.

father started the congregation at Trosper. Gilbert E. Chandler, a contemporary, remembered that J.W. did start both congregations. (In the list of congregations established by Masters, Appendix C, only the Artemus congregation is mentioned.)

Not long after his move to Barbourville, J.W. was engaged by some folks in Pineville to conduct a revival there in the county seat of adjoining Bell County. Perhaps the most significant convert in the Pineville revival was the first one. In his book, *Following the Trail*, he tells about this experience.

The most important meeting [at this time] was at Pineville, count-seat of Bell County. I began there Jan. 2, 1886. I stopped at the Bingham Hotel. I preached two weeks and organized a congregation. The Methodist circuit rider made headquarters there, but was out of town when I began. He was an Irishman. He came to town the second week of the meeting, and, having learned that several had made the confession, he went from house to house begging the people to stay away from the meeting. By the way, I had a larger crowd that night than before. He saw everybody else going, and he dropped in late.

After I closed my sermon I told him to say what he pleased to say. He got up and began: "Father Atkins was an Irishman and a Methodist preacher, and very fond of mush. He and a younger preacher were on their way to conference, and spent a night with a good sister who knew of Father Atkins' fondness for mush, so she took her bucket and went to the spring to get water to make the mush, and she happened to dip a frog up in the bucket. When supper was ready, the reverend gentleman sat down at the table, and the first dip that Father Atkins made he got the frog. The other Preacher saw what was in Father Atkins' plate, and said: 'Father Atkins, eat such as is set before you, asking no questions for conscience' sake.' 'Pshaw! do you think I can eat a frog for conscience' sake?' 'No, neither can I swallow the doctrine you have heard to-night for conscience' sake.'"

Then he leaped and jumped around and around. I wondered what I might say when he got through. I could not afford to reply to such foolishness, and I knew that the people present expected me to say something, Finally he quit, and as I arose I thought of what Paul said in Acts 17:30. I quoted, "'*The times of such ignorance God winked at,*' and I will just wink too, and adjourn." The Irishman said: "Do you call me a fool?" I answered: "You can take it just as it sounds to you."

Judge Moss' wife was my first convert in that meeting. Four others followed her the same night. The next morning the Judge came to the hotel and told me to get my baggage and go to his home and make it my home. From that day to the present, when in Pineville, Judge Moss's home is mine, and it is a pleasant one.

It was at the conclusion of this revival that Masters organized a church in Pineville. It was reported that while he was in Pineville, a Methodist circuit rider made house calls attempting to undermine him. The calls seemed to be of no avail. According to Masters' assessment, the minister's efforts were rather ineffective and he said he had "done no harm, and much good."

After this meeting I made my way to Harlan Courthouse, and preached a week or ten days there. Then up Cumberland River twenty-two miles and on the way I overtook an old woman on horseback. I said: "Good morning." She answered: "Howdy. What is your name?" I told her my name, and she said: "I guess you are the man who held the meeting in town." I told her I was the man. Then she said: "Mister, what desire do you belong to anyhow?" I said: "None." She responded "I thought all preachers belonged to some church." I replied: "I do belong to the church." "Well, what church?" I said the church of Christ. Then she said: "I didn't know that there were more than three churches — the Hardshell Baptist, the Missionary Baptist and the Methodist." I told her that the Lord had a church in the world. "Me and my old man are Baptists ourselves; do you believe in them?" I said: "No." "What do you believe in, then?" I answered: "The Lord." "Well, He is the main stone." I thought she was right in that. Just a few days before this, there was a storm across the mountain among the Kentucky hills, and the report was that two little boys were blown six miles. She referred to this, and said: "Do you believe it?" I said: "No," "Why, don't you know that there is nothing impossible with God?" I told her that I did not know that. "You a preacher and don't know that there is nothing impossible with God. You had better go home and read your Bible awhile longer." I said: "Let us look at it a little. Can God lie? Can God make two hills without a low place in the middle or between them?" "There are two things he can't do. Now, all I know about it is what my pastor says. Every time he preaches he says there is nothing impossible with God, and the next time I hear him say it I will call him down." From the bold front she put up to me I believe she would do just what she said she would.

Traveling back and forth from Fairview to Barbourville, J.W. became very familiar not only with the mountain trails and also with the mountain people. On one occasion as he rode over "the saddle of the Gap," (that is how the locals often referred to the Cumberland Gap in the Cumberland mountain range) he was delayed because his horse became lame. Never having met a stranger, he asked for lodging in the home of someone whom he did not know. This experience of mountain hospitality is in *Following the Trail.*

During the first three years of my work in Kentucky my home was in Virginia, eighty-five miles from Barbourville, Ky., and I met my appointment at the latter place monthly for three years, except one time, and was hindered that time by high water. On one occasion I was delayed on account of my horse being lame, caused by shoeing. I got across Cumberland Mountain down in the beautiful valley where Middlesboro is now located. About nine o'clock in the night the snow was six or eight inches deep. I saw a light shining dimly through a window on a hillside, some forty or fifty feet from the road. I rode up to the front and called for lodging at a stranger's home. The stranger took me in, and his good wife prepared a warm supper for me. I must say that among the grand old, sky-piercing mountains, around whose cragged heights the lurid lightnings have been playing with harmless fury for ages, live some of the most hospitable people under the sun. Yes, the stranger took me in. The next morning he traveled with me a few miles. I asked if he were a Christian and he said "No." I said: "You have some sweet little children that need the example of a Christian father. You have a good wife who needs the help of a Christian husband in training the children for usefulness and the higher life." He answered: "That is all true." "Why not, then, become a Christian?" I asked him. He said: "There are so many denominations I don't know which is right." I told him that I acknowledged that denominationalism is confusing in its tendency, but men, and not God, are responsible for its existence. Again I said: "Do you not know that there were Christians before denominationalism was thought of?" He answered: "Yes." "All right," I said. "You turn your back on denominationalism, with all its phases, and obey the Lord, and you will then be all that you need to be." We finally said "Good-bye." A few years afterward I met him again, and he informed me that he was an officer of the church of Christ, and thanked me for what he called the sermon in the saddle.

The Middlesboro congregation is my home church and from the first time I read about the preceding incident I have wondered about the identity of the man in the story. From an historical standpoint, it would have been helpful if J.W. Masters had not for the most part left out the names of people about whom he wrote. He often omitted names with the accounts of his traveling and preaching. Evangelizing was another matter. The event of a particular happening must have been what was important to him, and not names and such. After all, evangelism was enabling people to come to know Jesus Christ, and that was paramount to this mountain evangelist. Remembering all the details or giving particular attention to some of the incidentals like recording names or dates of various people or places was not always important. The same could be said for other kinds of incidentals too. Although the details of who, where and when were not given, the core information was. What happened was the point of telling incidences and accounts. That was how he told the following rather unusual story. "There was a log cabin by the roadside. To one corner a board was nailed extending over the road or path. On this board, were the words below: *'Hom maid shuggar and mun licker fur sail hear.'* I told this in a temperance speech at London, Ky., and the late Congressman Boring asked in what county this was. I said, 'None of your business,' and he said, 'Good!'"

In 1887 Masters organized a church in the Richlands section of Knox County. He called it the time when he "converted a

Baptist Church into a Christian Church." Later in his ministry, he returned to this church and was their regular Sunday preacher for a period of some two to three years.[7]

His monthly trips into Kentucky took him through Lee County, in Southwestern Virginia. His travels were always on horseback. His friend, Dr. Silas Shelburne, lived and practiced medicine in Lee County. Most likely, his medical practice was in the community of Rose Hill. Because of their friendship and continued contact through the years, it is possible that Dr. Shelburne was the one who promoted evangelistic meetings in the Rose Hill community for Brother Masters. It was reported that he preached there on one or more occasions. Under the leadership of Dr. Shelburne a congregation was established in Rose Hill.

Mr. Dave Stinson was a life long resident of Whitley County and a longtime member of the Whetstone Christian Church in the county. More than once I had the privilege of visiting with him. On one occasion, he spoke about his time and acquaintance with the Rose Hill community.

> I worked up there nearly three years. There was a fellow by the name of Wright who was there at the time holding a meeting. I was staying at a hotel there in Rose Hill and he came and said, "Let's go over to church tonight." I said, "What kind of a church?" He said, "A Christian Church." I said, "Yeah, one of these old Campbellite churches, I like to hear them. By the way, who organized this church?" He said, "J.W. Masters."

---

[7]   Years after J.W. Masters preached at the Richlands Church in Knox County, his son Shelburne H. Masters, also served as pastor there. In the late 1950s, while I was minister of First Christian Church in Williamsburg, I conducted a two-week revival at the Richlands Church. All through the years — whether in Virginia, Tennessee or Kentucky — it has been a nostalgic adventure for me to follow my great grandfather (and in this instance, also my great uncle) into the different communities and churches during my own ministry.

February 17, 1888,[8] is believed to be the birth date of Grandpa Masters' third and last son, Shelburne Hall Masters, of whom I have already made reference. He was named for J.W.'s beloved friend, Dr. Shelburne and a minister friend by the name of Hall.[9] Shortly thereafter the family moved from Virginia to Kentucky.

J.W. Masters had had three years of good preaching in Kentucky and, undoubtedly, during his pastorate in Barbourville made many contacts over many sections of the growing state. It was due to one of these contacts that he was given the call to Glasgow, Kentucky, as minister of the Christian Church. The precise time of this move, however, is not quite clear. Shelburne Masters was born February 17, 1888, in Fairview, Virginia. Accordingly, the family did not move until some time thereafter.

---

8   My Uncle Shelburne told me that one of his sisters had written in a Bible that he was born in 1889. Another, more complete record of 1888, however, was taken from the Bible of Mrs. W.J. Young, wherein is recorded birth dates of all the children of J.W. Masters.

9   In the interview with my Aunt Eunice Young, she said that her brother Shelburne was named for a "Brother Hall." It has been my understanding through the years that the name "Shelburne" came from Dr. Silas Shelburne's name. Very likely, this confirms and attests to his being named "Shelburne Hall Masters."

Days in Glasgow

Reverend Paul C. Duncan was minister of the First Christian Church, Glasgow over 50 years ago. I am indebted to the late Reverend Duncan for information from the records of that church.

Your [great] grandfather is listed with R.H. Crossfield and some other [ministers] that you will recognize. You will note also that there was a division in the church in 1889, and in 1890 a second church was established. It would seem from what I can find in the record books that your [great] grandfather led this division, taking a group out on Columbia Avenue and building another church.

I have two old record books — the one which seems to be the older of the two lists J.W. Masters and Mrs. J.W. Masters and it has "Fellowship withdrawn June 28, 1891." You will recall that in those days the preachers were not listed any differently than the members, and this listing does not call him an elder or minister or anything — it is just plain J.W. Masters.

In a later book that is dated 1890-1900, we have J.W. Masters and Mrs. J.W. Masters and a check mark indicating they removed by letter. However, the fascinating thing to you will be the action of the elders under the date of March 1890 wherein they give a list of some names. Your [great] grandfather is in the second part of folk who asked for their letters from the church. Instead of placing them in a Christian Church, they immediately established another congregation and were said to be, by

action of the elders, an insubordination. The elders
withdrew fellowship and the church concurred on
the date of April 13, 1890.[10]

As Reverend Duncan indicated, this material was of
considerable interest to me and is therefore included almost in
its entirety. Initially, I thought perhaps there was some scandal
in the congregation and my great grandfather was either
responsible for or a participant in some undesirable activity. Mr.
Duncan further stated that a Miss Hatty Myers — a member
of the Glasgow Church — told him, "The dispute was over the
authority of the elders, and came because of the use or the desire
to use stereopticon slides in the church." Apparently Mr. Duncan
interpreted the records, along with the comment from Miss
Myers, to mean Brother Masters was one of the liberal and open
minded preachers of the day who was willing to use the "magic
lanterns" for the spiritual good of the church. I remember well
one of the key issues in those days was a difference among many
congregations of the Stone-Campbell movement regarding the
use or non-use of musical instruments in the act of worship. So
volatile was this issue — as any church historian knows — in
1906 there was a church-wide division which resulted in the
emergence of two denominations: the Churches of Christ and
the Christian Church.

It may be that J.W. Masters led a group of the members of the
church in Glasgow into establishing another congregation where
they would be free to *"Speak where the scriptures speak, and remain
silent where the scriptures are silent."*[11] Obviously, as in other such
debates over the principle of congregational autonomy, some of
the members thought that anything not included in the text of

---

[10]   This information came from correspondence I had with the Reverend
    Duncan in January 1962. During several years in the 1950s Reverend
    Duncan and I were in summer youth church camp together. When he
    learned of my kinship with J.W. Masters, he agreed to send me material
    he had from early church records.

[11]   With the spread of the Stone-Campbell movement there were several
    slogans of this type among followers of this persuasion. This particular
    statement was a proposal made to the Christian Association of
    Washington, Pennsylvania on August 17, 1809, by Thomas Campbell.

the Bible should not be used in church matters. Others, however, held these matters to be in the realm of opinion. However it came about, the schism was not deep-rooted and did not last very long. According to Reverend Duncan, by 1902 the divisions were settled and the two congregations reunited.

Although it cannot be substantiated, from further records of the Glasgow Church at least one of J.W.'s brothers moved into the Glasgow area with him, or followed soon thereafter. It is believed Dave Masters and his wife Kate migrated — with their family — to Glasgow at that time. This statement is made on the strength of information found in two sources. One is from the Glasgow Sunday School Attendance Book of 1900-1901. Another is a record book dated 1894-99. Several persons by the name of Masters are listed in these records, including Kate Masters. Other members with the name Masters in the Glasgow records are not believed to be related to the J.W. Masters family.

Both Mrs. W.A. Parkey (my Aunt Lola) and Mrs. W.J. Young, (my Aunt Eunice) daughters of Grandpa Masters, say the family stay in Glasgow was for a relatively short time, approximately two years. When they made the move from Glasgow they returned to Southeastern Kentucky sometime in 1891, this time to Corbin.

One of the few references Masters made to his Glasgow pastorate was the following comment in regard to a revival he preached while he was there.

> While I was pastor at Glasgow, Ky., I was called about forty miles away to hold a meeting. When I reached the place the brethren told me that they were not expecting any additions. Just wanted the church warmed up. About one-half of the audience each night were Methodists and Presbyterians.
>
> After I had preached a week, I said: "To-morrow night I will tell you why our people don't sprinkle and pour water for baptism." I was making my home with one of the elders. The next morning another elder came, and the other one

went out for a talk. After a short time they both came into my room. The landlord said: "Brother Masters, we have decided that you had better not preach what you announced you would to-night." I answered: "All right; help me get my horse and buggy." "What are you going to do with them?" he asked. I said: "I will go home." "Say, we want the meeting to go on another week." I replied: "If I preach to-night, I will preach what I said I would." "Go ahead," he said. I asked then what was the matter with them. He said:. "This brother heard a Methodist brother last night say that you had the best interest here that had been for years, but you would bury it to-night so deep it will never be resurrected." I said: "All right, let her go. If the truth buries it, it ought to be buried."

That night the house and yard were filled. The two elders led the singing. When I called for the invitation song the two elders arose side by side, both using the same book. Then Methodists and Presbyterians began coming. The elders got excited and dropped the book on the table and quit singing. I said: "Sing on, brethren; it looks like more will come." They grabbed at the song-book and got the New Testament and sang on. Ten additions that night. I said: "It looks like something is buried sure enough." What was buried? Sprinkling. And in ten days I baptized thirty-five Methodists and Presbyterians. The elders begged my pardon and said that they were ashamed of themselves.

No other comment, either in his writing or in conversation in family circles, are there any further remarks about the Glasgow sojourn for the Masters extended family. Whether J.W. considered his brief ministry in Glasgow a success or failure is not known.

It is apparent the children of Henry and Sallie Masters (J.W.'s father and mother) were devoted to each other and kept as close as possible, both from a family sense and geographic location. I was informed by members of the family at various times one or more of J.W.'s brothers — with their families — followed him about the country, apparently to maintain the closeness of family ties. Within a few months after the birth of a daughter, Lola Elizabeth Masters, on August 15, 1890, the family moved from Glasgow to Corbin. There was a consensus among the Henry Masters children, they felt they had located the truly Happy Hunting Ground. When J.W., his sister, and his brothers — and their families — made the move to Corbin, the Masters clan deeply rooted themselves in the life and interests of that community. As mentioned earlier, the youngest child, daughter Nancy Eunice, was born in Corbin in 1891.

A College of Christian Learning

Being a former school teacher, J.W. Masters knew the need to get his children settled in school. After each family move, one of the first things he did was to find a school. Because there were few schools it was common in those days for families who had the means to do so to secure private tutoring for their children. This was not possible for J.W.'s family. His strong feeling about this need compelled him to do something about it. Since it was also a need for other children and young people in town and the neighboring communities, within a short time after the Masters' families moved to Corbin, J.W. conferred with a prominent Corbin businessman, David T. Chestnut. He discussed the possibility of starting a public school. He was aware of the need of his own children and equally concerned about the community's need for a college of Christian learning. As stated earlier, with the counsel and support of Mr. Chestnut, in the fall of 1891 the Corbin Academy was established. It was later known as Christian College.[12]

Articles in the Corbin Daily Tribune Newspaper say the Christian College, under the leadership of J.W. Masters and David Chestnut, was established in 1891. From the early history of the First Christian Church in Corbin, the record states the newly organized church met in the building of the Corbin Christian College.

The Corbin Daily Tribune newspaper carried a story in 1942, written by Dr. G. W. Campbell, about the Corbin school system.

> It seems from information given by old settlers that little or no interest was manifested in public school before 1896. The writer has failed to find any information concerning the public school of

---

[12] There is a street in Corbin named College Street. There must have been some association between the school and the name of the street. There has never been another "college" in the Corbin community.

Corbin prior to the establishment of Christian College, 1891. However it is definitely established that Mrs. Ada Gray Gilliam taught the "public school" in Christian College in 1894.

Both church and newspaper sources confirm the interest and subsequent establishment of this "college for learning" in Corbin.

Soon afterward the facilities of the college were made available to the city of Corbin for the use of public schooling. Another article appeared in the Corbin paper in 1951 regarding "Corbin's Early History."

> Dr. Campbell's research disclosed that there were no public schools in Corbin in buildings erected for such in the early days. He says the term of five months was taught in Christian College for both Knox and Whitley County students, but that the public school was separate and apart from the college.

With financial support from Mr. Chestnut, a two-story frame building was erected for the purpose of housing the school. The building which was located on East Main Street contained a chapel for religious services. Other than his interest and support at its beginning, Masters had little to no part in the day to day operation of the school. The booklet of the Fiftieth Anniversary of First Christian Church stated "the first church-sponsored school was called the Corbin Academy, later known as Christian College. This school was started in 1891 under the inspiration of Reverend J.W. Masters and David T. Chestnut."

In addition to the visibility of Masters in the new educational venture, there was also growing interest in the community regarding various occasions of his preaching. By the summer of 1892, he had generated considerable interest in this matter. The "Plea" he presented — what those who presented the principles of the Stone-Campbell movement called their message — was beginning to gain momentum. His preaching seemed to be attracting a number of people. Parenthetically, Corbin's estimated population at that time was about four hundred people. To gain support and attract as many from the community as he could, he did what he did best: he held a revival. By all numerical standards — then and now — the response was overwhelming. He considered this revival with the eighty-five additions to be the most successful revival he ever conducted.

According to his book, there were lots of additions in the revival. The congregation of the First Christian Church was organized by my great grandfather on August 6, 1892. There were only twenty-seven charter members, however, in organizing the church. Of this number, nine were members of the Masters family: J.W. Masters and wife, Henry Masters and wife, W.H. Masters and wife, D.A. Masters and wife, and Wilson Masters. (Unlike the pattern in recent years in new church establishment, children of these families were not included in the total number of charter members.) The Corbin Enterprise, a weekly newspaper founded only a few months prior to the establishment of the church, stated the church was organized at the Corbin Christian College.

It was evident that the popularity of the college had a wider base than was the attraction for the newly formed congregation. People outside town were interested in and contributed to the financial support of the college. Sheep and cattle were driven into town and auctioned off, and the proceeds given to the college. To handle these funds, trustees were appointed. The school and the congregation were so closely related, the leaders (apparently the trustees) of both the school and the church, were the same individuals.

The college and the church, both established under the leadership of the man they called Brother Masters, worked hand in hand. The building for the college was already on the East Side, so Masters moved his family to East Corbin. My Aunt Eunice told me about the early days of the new church:

> They would meet in the chapel and that is
> where my Daddy would preach. And Mrs. Gilliam
> (Ada Gray Gilliam, one of the charter members)
> said that the only music that they had was a

graphophone, phonograph we call it now.[13] And they would play records. This was all in the chapel of the school.

While Masters was serving as pastor of the church in Corbin, he began to preach at other points in that section of Southeastern Kentucky for the State Board of Missions of the Association of Christian Churches. Reports by the General Secretary of the State Board of Missions are in Bosworth Memorial Library of Lexington Theological Seminary. The following report is about J.W. Masters.

> In May, in 1893, J.W. noted in a small notebook which he carried with him that he had spent twenty-seven days out in the field; had preached twenty-eight sermons; had baptized five and received three others into the church. In June he had two additional appointments, as he called them. These two nights of preaching were on June 9th, at Scotts Schoolhouse, and June 13th, at Grays Station. From June to September he reported to the State Board that he had been in the field some sixty days, he had preached seventy-four sermons, and had had twelve additions by baptism.

Seeing that his work in evangelism was continuing to grow, Masters decided to terminate his pastorate with the Corbin Christian Church and devote more time in his evangelistic work in Southeastern Kentucky. For the next several years, however, he maintained his residence in Corbin and his family remained there while he traveled into adjoining counties. It was in September of 1893 J.W. officially closed his ministry with the Corbin church. Until that time the church was still meeting in the chapel of the college. The church records show that under Masters guidance

---

[13] The graphophone instrument was invented in 1886, according to *The New Century Dictionary*. The use of this rather new innovation further indicates Masters' progressive spirit and willingness to use anything he felt necessary and helpful to further the cause of the church as long as its use was not contrary to the spirit and intent of the scriptures.

the church flourished and for a period of time had the largest membership of any church in town.

According to *Fifty Years in the Faith*, the school building burned December 24, 1899. The date of the fire is in question, but from articles in the Corbin Daily Tribune, as well as information in the Official Minutes of the Board of Directors of the Kentucky Christian Missionary Convention in 1897, the consensus is the building burned on December 24, 1897.

> [The fire occurred during the time when] J.W. Hawkins was holding a meeting. Mr. Gastineau's son was janitor. He filled a lamp with oil and lighted it. In trying to place the lamp in a bracket on the wall, he let it slip from his hands. It rolled down the stairs, spilling burning oil as it rolled. The building was a total loss.

The loss of this building, both for the use of the school and the congregation, was a terrible blow. Because of insufficient funds to rebuild the facility, the school suffered the most and was not re-established. The church made alternate arrangements and continued its efforts in providing ministry to the small number of families it nurtured.

The Demands and Cost of Fulfilling a Dream

With Masters' growing reputation as an acclaimed speaker came additional responsibilities. Accordingly, his travel schedule increased considerably due to his preaching for the Kentucky State Board of Missions. He had a growing desire to do evangelistic preaching as well as pastoral work. During the latter part of his pastorate of the Corbin congregation he traveled to Harlan County. It is not known when he first ventured into the Harlan territory. During these journeys he began to make contacts for the work of the State Board. On one trip he contacted several men in a congregation in Harlan County who agreed to give various amounts of financial support for his work. Whether or not such information was shared with other members of the congregation is not known. The contract was written in a small notebook Masters carried in his coat pocket. (My cousin, and J.W. Masters' grandson, Marion Parkey, gave me the notebook during the time of my initial research in 1961 and 1962.)[14] The arrangement was to become effective in November of 1893. According to the initial wording, the agreement was secured in September a few months prior to the starting of the contract in November. Following the explanation of the agreement is the list of the names of the men who made the commitment. The amounts of money are unbelievably smaller than the smallest amount of support of any minister today. The total amounted

---

[14] Marion and I are both descendants and recipients of the legacy of J.W. Masters. His mother Lola and my grandmother Sallie were daughters of J.W. and Rebecca. Marion is an ordained minister in the Christian Church. He gave the Ordination Prayer when I was ordained in 1956, at the First Christian Church of Middlesboro. With the exception of one venture into Humboldt, Tennessee, Marion has spent his entire ministry in Kentucky. Like his grandfather before him, he too spent most of that time in Southeastern Kentucky. One of the congregations he served was the Christian Church in Mount Vernon, in Rockcastle County. That simply indicates he, too, has shared some common experiences with this "standing-tall-sitting-high-in-the-saddle-mountain-preacher-grandfather" just the same as I have.

to $35 for a whole month. No one will ever know whether or not on those lonely horseback journeys into the mountains, if J.W. Masters ever thought how different it could have been, how much easier it could have been, how much more profitable it could have been for him and his family had he [1] yielded to his father-in-law's desires for him to become part of the established Baptist church, and thus enjoy a rather comfortable lifestyle. Or [2] what it might have been like had he chosen to stay with either of the two alternative pursuits he had considered — law and medicine. Such questions today are pure imagination. The total of $35 for an entire month is listed to show the commitment of these individuals who wanted the ministerial services of Brother Masters; and to indicate the kind of sacrifice J.W. made and how difficult it was for him to provide for his family.

> Harlan, Ky. Sept. 23-93. We the undersigned agree to pay the amts [amounts] opposite our names for the services of J.W. Masters as an evangelist at Harlan Ky. Monthly for one year beginning third Lord's day — Nov. 1893.

J. J. Hopkins	3.00
J. G. Forrester	5.00
S. Z. C. Howard	7.00
H. L. Howard	10.00
F. G. Lussn	10.00

On the opposite side of the page of the small notebook which contained the above information is a simple item of subtraction. There is the listing of 1893 minus 1854. There is another figure, showing 39 as the number. The indication is clear and merely is a reminder that at the time of the entry into his notebook, J.W. Masters was thirty-nine years old.

Masters' heart was so full of zeal and desire to spread the Restoration Plea with folks near and far, he rarely concentrated on only one emphasis or in one place at a time. While he preached regularly in the Harlan "pastorate" on behalf of the State Board, he conducted a revival in his home community of Corbin. Part of the measurable results, were 34 additions to the church.

The ministerial duties and services of J.W. Masters to the entire Corbin community over a period of some thirty-plus years crisscrossed numbers of times. Moving to and from Corbin over the latter part of his 70 years so identified him with that town and the residents within and around its borders, at times it is hard to picture him associated anywhere else.

Mountain Memories

Masters' trips to the mountains were more than occasional but less than routine. He described one particular trip where he shared the companionship of an elderly preacher. The incident makes it quite evident that throughout his travels in the Kentucky mountains, the ministry to which J.W. Masters ascribed consisted primarily of strong preaching and frequent baptisms. This story so indicates.

> Some years ago I was going up into the mountains, and came to the home of an old preacher, who went with me about thirty miles. He was a very good singer of the old kind. One cold morning there were four persons to be baptized. The old preacher said: "Who will do the baptizing, or will we both do it?" I answered: "No need of both going in the water to do that little work. They may have a choice to have some one to see them." So he sent a man into the house to investigate, who came out saying: "They want Brother Masters." The old preacher turned away saying: "I don't care." The next one to be baptized was a woman eighty years old, a relative of the old preacher. I told him to get ready and baptize the old lady. He went into the swift water with her and it looked like he meant to baptize her head downstream. I spoke, saying: "Turn your back upstream."[15] He said: "No use of that." He said the words, and it seemed that he tried to press her

---

[15] In my student pastorate in Clinchport, VA, before my first baptism there, Aunt Rose Miller gave me that same advice. She knew that a young minister who had never before baptized someone in a moving river wouldn't know the "upstream" and "downstream" rules of baptizing. Obviously, folks in mountain and rural areas like my Grandpa and Aunt Rose all know there is a difference in baptizing in running water and baptizing in a baptistery.

down and let the water pass over her. She pulled away from him, throwing herself upstream, really baptizing herself. The preacher took her arm and lifted her to her feet, started to the bank and let her fall, and said: "Did you ever see the beat of that?" I said: "No, and I don't want to." The old preacher responded: "She was the hardest woman to make squat I ever baptized in my life." Poor fellow! Never mentioned it to me after that, and never proposed baptizing any others.

Prior to his involvement in any official establishment of the congregation in Harlan, much preliminary work was done by this horseback riding evangelist during the last decade of the nineteenth century. Any conversation with Mr. Dave Stinson about J.W. Masters left the impression Mr. Stinson was very confident in what he was relating. He said these early preaching occasions were held in the Harlan Court House. In those days there was little concern for any breech of the principle of separation of church and state. That had to do with (revival) meetings whether they were held in government buildings or school facilities. Whether the occasion was for a revival and hence, worship or for a religious debate, the use of public and government property at that, court houses were frequently used for such events. Stinson described Masters' time in Harlan.

J.W. Masters organized Harlan town. And there's where he had so much trouble with the Baptists taking our churches because one of them outlaws[16] didn't want him to preach. Back then, that was rougher than any country. I have heard him tell it many-a-time. One day somebody gave him a big heavy walking cane. He said the next morning he got out and started down the street.

---

[16] It is quite evident Mr. Dave Stinson had no hesitancy about showing his feelings or his religious bias in using language to describe something or someone. He was very transparent and made no attempt to camouflage whatever he was thinking. As the saying goes, he wore his feelings on his sleeve.

As he walked along a fellow said, "Well, Brother Masters, what are you going to do with that stick? It looks like it might come in handy today." He [Masters] said, "Well, I hadn't planned on anything like that. But a man could push me and make me."[17]

By the time Masters had completed his allotted time of one year in Harlan on behalf of the State Board, he agreed to keep regular appointments. At the same time, he further agreed to serve the church in London. A conversation with Mrs. Logan Ewell provided some vivid recollections of those days.

J.W. Masters of Corbin came to us January 1895 and served two years, until December 1897. It was during the term of J.W. Masters that I joined the church. I was baptized by Brothers Masters, May, 1895. I was 11 years of age at the time. At this age I begun to take notice of the sermons preached in our churches and while I held Brother Masters in high esteem for his character and gentle demeanor I was not so particularly impressed by his sermons, which, as I recall, did not appeal to one so young as I. He did, however, persuade me to join the church.

The testimony of Mrs. Ewell stands out as an isolated comment among the many statements to the contrary about Brother Masters' strong preaching. There is no need to attempt to rise to the defense of his preaching. In any event, she acknowledged that hers was the impression of one quite young. It is probable

---

17   Mr. Stinson thought Masters organized the church in Harlan. On the other hand, I received information from Mr. "Doc" Sullivan, who said this congregation was started right after the Civil War, about 1868. It is likely that J.W. Masters either revived the church or reorganized it. Through the years this has not been a strong church and has struggled at times to maintain its ministry in the community where coal mining has been the principle source of employment for many families. During his ministry, Masters revived and reorganized many churches. The Harlan congregation may have been one of those churches.

other youth might have made the same observation. Her words did fortify the essence of that preaching: it was persuasive and effective toward the end to get one to accept Christ and unite with the church. In that regard he was most successful.

The Masters family lived in London for a short time, but in the spring of 1897 returned to Corbin where they established residence in the east part of town on a street that is today known as Masters Street. My Aunt Lola told me the street was so named because of the number of Masters families who have lived there through the years. The house into which J.W. and Rebecca moved their family belonged to his friend D.T. Chestnut. It had been built by another close friend, W.P. Durham, a resident of Corbin. According to a letter J.W. sent to Durham, by the time the Christian Church was organized in Corbin, Mr. Durham had moved to Preachersville, Kentucky in Rockcastle County. In the letter dated April 22, 1897, J.W. expressed to Durham his worry and troubled spirit. Apparently his concern was over the move from London back to Corbin.

> I have been involved in a great deal of trouble and worry this spring. My wife became so badly dissatisfied in London that I had to move back to Corbin. I now live in the house that you Bro. D. built for Mrs. Chestnut. Will live there till I get my house built. I am building on my farm — a two story. I am very greatly pressed financially, but hope that all will work out for the best in this event.[18]

My Aunt Eunice told me that her father bought a piece of property on the Barbourville Road, in East Corbin. The house was behind where now the St. Camilla Catholic School is located.

---

[18] This kind of letter J.W. sent to friends from time to time contained information about him, his family, and also their ever present financial struggles. It could have been his intent that such letters served a two-fold purpose: [1] give general information; [2] let the recipient know of his continuing financial needs, thus making a non-verbal appeal for support to those friends who so often had let him know of their interest in providing him such assistance when needed.

Since there was more to the property than merely a house and grounds, he called this his farm.

In June of that year Masters began to expand his range of preaching locations. He was engaged to conduct a revival in Booneville, Ky. En route he stopped and preached one night in McKee. The London newspaper, *Mountain Echo*, carried two very favorable articles regarding the large crowds and excellent preaching at both places.

I had an interview with Mr. Andrew J. Walker, editor of the Corbin Daily Tribune weekly newspaper. He told me about a debate that took place either in the summer of 1896 or 1897.

> J.W. Masters debated with Rev. William Estes in London. It was likely to have been at the Court House or the school house. Preacher Estes was a Baptist. All of the Baptists and Methodists were pulling for Estes and all of the rest were for Masters. The issue of the debate was concerning the doctrine of the two churches. I didn't attend the debate, but I remember hearing that in the debate Estes said that Masters' doctrine "wasn't worth any more than a frost-bitten pumpkin in the fall of the year." Everybody talked about it. [Later there was a second debate between Brother Masters and William Estes.]

By this time in his ministry, J.W. Masters continued to carry a heavy load of responsibilities which accompanied his preaching for the State Board. It is easy to determine, though, his interests never varied from nor did he cease to accept challenges in defending his faith. Opportunities to proclaim, promote and defend his faith came both in his preaching and in his debating.

Whetstone Christian Church

During the summer of 1897, Masters preached at several churches in Southeastern Kentucky. Before he concluded his ministry with the London congregation in December, he preached at the Whetstone Christian Church.[19] Some folks like longtime member Dave Stinson and the Reverend Ashley Garland, minister of the congregation, occasionally referred to the Whetstone congregation informally and called it *Whetrock* Christian Church. Mr. Stinson reflected on his youth and the influence Brothers Masters had on him.

> I think he must have held his first meeting there somewhere during the time I was just a boy. He had been preaching at Woodbine [just outside Corbin] and some child died on Meadow Creek, down in the Sharp Settlement there. Bro. Masters came down there and preached that funeral. And some of 'em heard him, you know, and asked him why he couldn't come to Whetrock and preach. He says, "I can." And he came down there and held this meeting, but to my best recollection he didn't get very many additions at that time. But he come back again about the following year and got forty the next time.

---

[19] Whetstone Christian Church is located in a rural part of Whitley County and is surrounded by several acres of land. In the fall of 1957, I held my first of several revivals at the Whetstone Church. I was told of the crowds my great grandfather drew when he preached there. One man in the church told me that the whole area around the church facility was covered with horses and wagons and people. No doubt it was. (Several times I have remarked that whereas they came in droves for my great grandfather's preaching, when it was announced that I was to preach... they stayed away in droves.) The man also said — which I thought was somewhat of an exaggeration — at some meetings there must have been 5,000 people in attendance. Through the years, as I have learned of the immense popularity and drawing power of this evangelist, I thus have come to accept such comments with more credibility than I did early on. Moreover, it is reminiscent of the Revivalism of the nineteenth century, particularly as it relates to the crowds that came from miles around to attend the Cane Ridge Revival in Bourbon County in 1804.

About 1901, he held one meeting about a month long. Now they just come there in wagons, and buggy, and horseback. Even come from Woodbine down there, off Poplar Creek. I was getting to be a pretty good-sized lad then. My mother and daddy joined them that time. They weren't baptized at a regular baptizing; they just told him, "Now you come down to the house, there's a river right over from the house and we'll just go over there and be baptized and then come on back to the house." Back in those days it was hard for a preacher to find a place to study. So Dad told him, "Just go and get your grip, and as long as I have a house, you have a house." And from that time on, he just about made his headquarters there. Every time he'd come he'd drive in there, and I'd kid him and tell him he'd drive a poor horse down there and leave with a fat one.[20]

J.W. Masters on Horse

---

[20] This is a picture of Masters on his horse. He once said to someone that during his ministry, he had worn out 4 horses

He'd go to the river every day and carry him a big load of horse weeds to feed that horse. And if he stayed there two weeks it'd look like a different horse when he left. He was a wonder. And to think that no more education than he had — just looks like he was an inspired man

The meetings held by J.W. Masters at the Whetstone Christian Church were frequent through the years. The ties he made there were strong and lasting. His relationship to the Whetstone Church and the friendships he formed there later provided some significant events for his overall ministry.

During my visits and occasions for preaching at Whetstone in the late 1950s, several of the older members were quite anxious to talk to me about my great grandfather. They thought of him fondly and still regarded him with great respect. It sometimes occurred to me their interest in having me come to preach for a revival at Whetstone at the various times I did, was most likely due to the fact that John Masters was my great grandfather. Out of respect and memory for him they showed equal respect and appreciation for my preaching and friendship while I was minister in Williamsburg. It is also possible they held out the hope that what happened at his occasions of preaching just might happen again during my preaching visits with them.

Challenges, Counter Challenges and A Touch of Humor

Masters remembered a time when he had been engaged to preach during a revival in a school house. At the conclusion of his sermon, he was challenged by a person in attendance.

> I had an appointment on the head of a creek to preach, beginning Wednesday night and continuing until Sunday. The Methodist people had a little organization worshiping in the schoolhouse. When I arrived in the neighborhood I was told that one of the Methodist brethren had gone to town and got his preacher to begin at the same place on Thursday night, and continue until Sunday. So, when I closed my sermon Wednesday night and announced preaching for the following night, the Methodist brother arose, saying: "Our preacher will be here to-morrow night and remain until Sunday." "All right," I answered; "I can stand him as long as he can me, and I guess you will find it that way." This fellow went away threatening to lock me out. Sure enough, the preacher was on the ground the next night, but I could not get him to work. The next day the man who had threatened to lock me out, and three or four other men, were making a dam in the creek to baptize a man and his wife who had joined the Methodist Church in a previous meeting and would not be sprinkled. I rode along by and said: "Men, you ought to baptize the man who talks about locking me out." The man said: "I am the fellow." "Well," I said, "I beg your pardon. A man ought not to be baptized until he is a better man than you are." None of them laughed.

Friday night the preacher was on hand again, but would not say anything. Saturday morning we had a good crowd, and the preacher asked me to let him preach first. I did so. He took the floor with his Bible and *Discipline* both in hand, and tried to prove that the *Discipline* was a necessity along with the Bible. After he was done he took his seat with the Bible on his knee. I arose, saying: "Brother, your *Discipline* says we are justified by faith only, and your Bible says we are not justified by faith only; which do you want your people to believe — your *Discipline* or your Bible, they can't believe both." Just then he said, "I am going home," and got up and left. That night the door was locked. Sunday morning a man, whose life I had saved from being shot to death,[21] took a forty-five out of his trunk and shot the lock off the door. And I had a good crowd to preach to that morning. From there I went in the afternoon, about six miles to another place, held a ten days' meeting, and baptized several people.

This kind of incident involving two ministers from two denominations preaching at virtually the same time and/or in the same place is certainly not customary today. Perhaps, even then such a practice happened only in the mountain communities. A public challenge and counter challenge by ministers during a revival was obviously something that would and did draw a crowd. One hopes that the purpose of such antics was not merely to draw attention or attendance.

A family by the name of Jones was very close to the J.W. Masters family, both of whom lived in Corbin. The Joneses

---

21   Sometimes comments such as this one that are not explained say about as much as if there had been commentary with them. Here is a simple reference to an occasion when John Masters saved a man from being shot and killed. And then he makes no further remarks and gives no further details. The incident obviously left such an impression upon the man himself that he was willing to use his gun and make it possible for this preacher to have a place to preach. Interesting!

moved to Rogersville, Tennessee. The month after he concluded his ministry in London, J.W. received an invitation to visit these friends in their new Rogersville location and conduct a revival. He tells an interesting story connected with the revival. The story is rather lengthy but worth telling in its entirety. It indicates how J.W. used humor effectively, answering ridicule with ridicule. Masters felt he needed to respond to an editorial in the local newspaper by the editor whereby he was criticized for his style of preaching. He told a story in which he associated the subject with the editor and called him an *unfinished man.*

> Brother Jones and wife wrote me to go over to Rogersville and preach for them. They were the only two of our people in the town. I landed into that town on Jan. 8, 1898. There were four church-houses in the town, but the doors were locked against me. Finally I got the court-house and began the meeting.[22] The first night I had about two dozen colored people and as many white. Jones was discouraged, but I was not, I answered questions. A denominational preacher would say: "I will put a question to-night that will swamp him." Of course, every one hearing of this went to see me "swamped." My audience got larger and larger, until the house was filled to its capacity. In three weeks [about the first of February, 1898] I organized a congregation of fifty-three people.
>
> Among others I baptized a saloon-keeper's daughter, and one morning I was passing the saloon and the keeper hailed me. He came out with the County paper (The *Hawkins County Star*) in his hand and as mad as tucker. He said, "Have

---

[22] Apparently the matter of securing a place for preaching was often necessary. Obviously, it was the job of someone to secure a location for a preaching appointment or revival. From comments Masters made, it would certainly appear that often it fell to his responsibility to make such arrangements.

you seen this?" showing me an article. I said:
"What about it, anyway?" "Well," he said, "look
at what the editor has said about you." It was real
funny. The editor said that I was preaching "water
salvation Antediluvian flood baptism." "All right,"
I said. I went up into another part of the town and
my friends were rowdy. I told the men to be quiet
— "That article is the best thing I have seen since
the meeting began. We will get good out of it."

That night a question was put on the bench
asking what I thought of the editor and what
he said about me. I read the query out loud and
looked at the editor. He smiled. I said: "It is not
fair to have a man tell what he thinks of another
every time, but in this case I can very well afford
to tell what I think of the editor. In the first place,
I think he is a good fellow; and second, I think he
is a sensible follow; and in the third place, I think
he thinks so too." The crowd laughed. "Now, that
is all I think about the editor tonight. But I beg
your pardon. I must tell you what I was reminded
of this morning when I saw the paper. It was
this. There was a man who did not have as much
common sense as you men have. He played with
the boys, and the boys told him that the first man
was made of mud. The man said: "If any man was
ever made of mud, I can make one." So he began,
and worked about a week, and told the boys he
would finish his man in the morning. During
the night the boys hid the mud man. The next
morning he went into his workshop and saw his
man had gone. "You had your man nearer done
than you thought; he has walked off and left you.
You will find him around here somewhere." So
he lit out hunting his man. He saw another man
passing down the street hurriedly; he fell in behind

the man, thinking he was his man, and finally the man said; "What in the blazes are you following me for?" "What made you run off before you were finished," he said. Little did I think that this man had gotten over here, and was the editor of the *Hawkins County Star*, until this morning." No smile from the editor then.

That night I went home with Dr. Morgan... The next morning the doctor said: "Brother Masters, you keep your seat. I want to see the editor before you go out in town, I believe he got mad last night." I said; "Doctor, I did nothing to make him mad, and I will go and see." I had a nice walking-stick a man had made for me, and I got the stick and started, and, behold, the first man I saw was the editor standing on the public square. I said; "Good morning, Colonel." He said: "Good morning. Stop there, parson," making his way toward me. I waited, but I did not want to wait. I sure thought that I was going to get into it with him... I watched his face, and at last he smiled. I never was as proud of a smile in my life as I was then. Gee, but I was glad! The editor said: "Here is your unfinished man. I will acknowledge that I foolishly got mad last night, but after I thought over the matter I was so well tickled I could hardly sleep. The boys want me to come back at you next week, but I said no, that I began it and that you finished it." The next week he wrote up the meeting in fine style, advising people to go and hear the old Jerusalem gospel preacher.

Much of the time most folks reasoned that Brother Masters had a purpose and a goal in mind when using his quick and genuine humor. Apparently, the occasions he offended folks with his humor were few and far between. J.W. Masters was a master in knowing how to use humor. Genuine humor and its use is a world apart from telling jokes just "to warm up a crowd." He saw humor where perhaps others did not. There will be many times we will note the intent of Masters' use of humor. Indeed, he used it to make a point or to convey a message.

Sometimes, however, attempting to find humor in a setting just does not work. At best it fails and at worst it backfires. Masters' next episode more or less falls into that category.

> I called at a tavern one night after dark; supper was over. While I was eating, the landlord put my horse away. After eating, I went to the front room, and there sat an old man who had just come in. He was as drunk as a loon. I introduced myself to him and he said: "Is this the preacher?" I said: "Yes." "Well, who was the Lord talking to when he said, 'Let us make man'?" I answered: "His Son, I suppose." "That is the difference in a man who knows things and the man who knows nothing; but, brother, when I go to bed at night I know that, if I die before morning, I will go right up to heaven," was his next statement. He made the statement, slobbering like a mad dog. I laughed. He said: "You must think I have no religion." "Not much," I said. He then said: "That is the way of a man, when he has no religion himself he thinks nobody else has any." Do you suppose I laughed any more?

Revivals, Revivals

Not long after he returned from Rogersville, Masters made a trip to the Shepherdsville community beyond central Kentucky to conduct a revival. A seminary colleague of mine, the Reverend Robert Bray, did his student ministry at the Shepherdsville Christian Church. I asked Bob about their church records and he did some research and told me that the records reported that J.W. Masters had organized a Christian Church there. The year the church was organized was 1898, the same year in which he organized the Rogersville church.

That same year Masters was again called back to the Whetstone Church in Whitley County to conduct another revival. On a hot August afternoon I sat in the shade and conducted an interview with Mr. "Doc" Sullivan who lived outside Corbin. He told me that it was at the revival that year when he first heard J.W. Masters preach. As I have reported earlier, the association of these two men served them both for many years.

> That year the meeting at Whetstone was a long one. At this meeting the wife of the old man who lived in the bend of the road joined. She was a small woman. And he didn't like it because she joined and he sent word to J.W. and said that he'd better not baptize his wife, because he'd be there with a shotgun. He just sent him word back and said, "Brother, you just tell him to come on, and bring his shotgun; if his wife wants to be baptized, I will baptize her." And everybody was just standing on the edge of the bank to see what was going to take place, and he never did show up.

The following year, in 1899, J.W. Masters held a revival in a neighboring city, Jellico, Tennessee. Half of this small community is in Whitley County, Kentucky and half is in Campbell County, Tennessee. My father-in-law, Judge J.B. Johnson, Sr., grew up in Whitley County. Not only did he know many of the people mentioned in my writing of the life of J.W. Masters, but being a public figure, he obviously was well acquainted with most residents in each of the mountain communities. The information about the following Jellico incident was given to him by Mrs. W.J. Beale of Jellico. She informed him that the Jellico revival in question was held in the City School Auditorium. As a result of the revival they organized a Christian Church. Lots of times, when there is good news there is bad news. Not too many years before this time, in the early days of the Corbin church, a tragic fire destroyed it and its contents. Similarly, not long after the beginning of the Jellico church, fire destroyed it. My father-in-law told me what he learned about the fire from Mrs. Beale.

In 1904 the members of this new Christian Church which had been organized by Bro. Masters only a few years previously, bought a lot and soon began to construct a new church building. It was completed in the summer of 1906. Within 30 days it was practically destroyed by the now famous and historic "Jellico Explosion." This occurred September 21, 1906, about 8 o'clock in the morning. Eight people were killed, several hundred injured, and thousands of dollars of property destroyed. In switching from one train track to another, a box car of dynamite hit another car and caused the explosion. It didn't take the members of the church long to determine that they would rebuild. R.G. Sherrer was the pastor at the time when the explosion occurred and during the time of the rebuilding that followed.

One of the things that endured Brother Masters to those to whom he preached, those to whom he ministered, and those whom he loved, was the fact that he frequently maintained contact with churches which he had organized. Desiring to keep in close contact with the churches where he had been was nothing new, particularly since this was the style of caring adopted by the Apostle Paul. Accordingly, Brother Masters followed this principle, keeping in touch with the folks in Jellico. Years later, Mrs. Lila Masters remembered he not only returned to preach for the Jellico congregation, but also for churches in neighboring communities. He preached both for the church at Jellico and also for the church at Procter Mines, a small mountain community near Jellico.

The War-Horse

In the spring of 1899, Masters was challenged to a debate with Dr. W.S. Culveyhouse, a Methodist layman whom his fellow-churchmen called their "war-horse." (His nickname speaks lots about the reputation he had gained for his exploits at debating.) Not long before this, the "war-horse" had engaged in a debate with one of the younger men of the Christian Church. He was obviously encouraged by the success he achieved and felt confident as a result of what he considered a victory. Dave Stinson remembered the debate.

> Now that was one of the awfulest crowds you've ever seen, that big house was full just as long as they could jam one in there and they were standing around at every window. It was the most enthused crowd I believe I ever saw. They just hollered and hooped and yelled — it was a sight. After each fellow would finish his speech, they would carry on so. Of course, Culveyhouse wasn't a deep-read man. I knew him a long time after that. He was an old-time doctor. And J.W. could just handle him with all ease. Wayne Bradley and A.J. Karr were the judges. Wayne was a Methodist and A.J. was a Christian preacher.

> Then they got on to sprinkling. And J.W. told him what the Bible was on it. He poured him out a glass of water from the pitcher that was there. J.W. then dipped his finger down in the water and just flipped it over on Culveyhouse and said to him, "Brother, I baptize you." He was as antic as he could be and he had an answer for everything that come and he didn't have to think about it. After that, Wayne never came back to the church. But whenever J.W. would come back and preach, he

wanted a seat right on the front. And he'd just sit there; I do not care if he had make him sick, every sermon that J.W. Masters preached, Wayne Bradley was there.

During the debate with Dr. W.S. Culveyhouse, after Masters had made a point, there was a man in the audience that asked, "Brother Masters, is that scripture?" Masters replied, "Where were you born?" Masters stated to my father that if he had known that Culveyhouse had not known more about the subject, then he wouldn't have accepted the debate. The judges gave the debate in favor of Masters.

At times things are said by the two proponents in a debate which seem to offer viewpoints and comments shrouded with good humored ridicule and sarcasm. At other there times, it is as though comments are exchanged for the sake of pure ridicule and sarcasm. There is a hint of that flavor in Masters' account of the same debate. Whereas Stinson gives names and says the debater was Dr. W.S. Culveyhouse, Masters simply gives the essentials which interested him.

I was called to debate with what the Methodists called their "war-horse," who had just a short while before had a debate with one of our younger preachers and thought he had gained a victory. I made the first speech, and the "war-horse" got up saying: "My brethren have had me half scared; they told me that Masters would eat me up, but since I have heard him I am not afraid of it." I said: "No, you need not be uneasy about that, for nothing common or unclean ever enters my mouth." So we had what the boys used to call a "hog-killing time." The second day at noon the "war-horse" quit. One old Methodist said: "If we had known this, we would have had a bigger gun; we have bigger ones." Then one of our old brethren said: "Your gun is all right, but your ammunition is not good." I have never heard of the "war-horse" debating any more. Perhaps he has learned that his "ammunition" is no good.

Once I was called eighteen miles from Corbin to preach a funeral in a Methodist neighborhood. After the funeral services the Methodist people asked me to preach another sermon, I agreed to do so, and made my second sermon fit the funeral occasion as well as I could. We had perhaps a half-dozen people in that section. They were advised by the Methodists to have me go back and hold a meeting. I went back in a few weeks, preached ten days in the Methodist church-house, and captured thirty-five of the Methodist people.

J.W. Masters was most certainly not a small-spirited person who just happened also to be a proclaimer of the gospel. He fought as valiantly for the unity of the church as any ecumenist has done then or now. Yet the ecclesiastical atmosphere in those early days must have been every much as collegial and well-intended as ours. While the prickly barbs and sometimes sharp comments which passed from theological position to theological position, from church to church, and from debater to debater, seems harsh to us, I firmly believe it was done in an open and honest exchange between strong proponents and servants of God. I offer such comments in reference to the previous story regarding the funeral and in light of the next. Both are from *Following the Trail*.

I went into a town and saw a Baptist preacher, a friend of mine, talking to a stranger. I said, "Who is this man?" and my friend answered, "This is our new pastor," giving his name. I shook hands with him, stepped back and said: "I have just done something that Paul never did in his life." "What

was that!" asked the stranger. I replied: "Shook
hands with a Baptist preacher." He said: "Was not
Paul one?" I answered: "If he was, he never let
anyone know it." The new pastor got angry, talking
boisterously, I walked on and left him blowing.

Verbal exchanges between men like my great grandfather
and his contemporaries in the late 19th and early 20th centuries
are examples of dialogue which we don't experience in this
time. In addition, phrases which they used seem strange to the
ecumenically-minded in our time. There is a common word
which virtually saturates the next couple of comments. The
times and locations of these circumstances is neither significant
nor the point. One word stands out and sets apart a particular
concept. I have added the italics in the following statements for
emphasis.

- "In one meeting at the mouth of a creek I thought that it was
  a great revival, as I had *captured* twenty-three Baptists, one
  being a preacher."
- "I continued the meeting a week longer, baptized twenty-four
  and *captured* twenty-four Baptists. I went away rejoicing
  over truth's victory."
- "I went back in a few weeks, preached ten days in the
  Methodist church-house, and *captured* thirty-five of the
  Methodist people."

It is interesting — and more than a little perplexing — that
"*captured*" is the word both Mr. Masters and Mrs. (Lila) Masters
used in describing how folks from other churches (denominations)
became members of the Christian Church. Parenthetically, my
Grandpa Masters didn't like and most certainly would not have
used the word "denomination" to refer to his church. Being part
of the *non-denominational Christian Church / Church of Christ* was
very basic to who he was, how he saw himself and his church
and how he spoke in promoting the Restoration Plea and the
cause of Jesus Christ. In my interview with Mrs. Masters, not
surprisingly she used the same term. Today no pastor, minister or

preacher that I know would use the language *"capture"* in referring to what my great grandfather and his colleagues intended and regarded to be the same idea: transfer of membership (and perhaps rededication). Today the transitions of folks changing from one church to another and references thereto are a lot softer in both language and concept. I'm confident, however, that the intent "then" is similar or identical to "now" regarding the same transactions of membership exchange. The term *"capture"* just carried a stronger sense of victory.

In the summer of 1899, the Masters family moved from their Corbin farm on the Barbourville Road to Keavy, Kentucky. My Uncle Shelburne told me after they moved he and one of his sisters were involved in a rather humorous incident. That is, they thought it was funny; but their father did not.

> My mother was very weakly and my father got a woman nearby, at Craig's Creek, to do our washing. We were living in Keavy in Laurel County. Craig's Creek is about a mile away. She had two or three little girls. My sister and I would go down there and while the lady was doing the washing we'd have services and I'd do the preaching. I'd get up on a rock and preach and then I'd take them down to the creek and baptize them. One day my father slipped down there and I was preaching about John the Baptist. And I said he was dressed in *"Campbellite* hair." My father walked in behind me and said, "Now, son, that's enough of that. I'll make you think *Campbellite* hair!" And he broke up my meeting that day and I didn't even baptize my converts.

To my Uncle Shelly, although humor was one of the arrows in his father's quiver, he reasoned that such an incident caught his father by surprise and thus, he did not share his children's sense of humor in the "pretend" baptism.

Finances

Throughout this account I have made reference to the constant concern J.W. Masters gave to finances. There is no complete record indicating how much financial support he received from the churches either he served or for whom he preached. Periodically, however, in the minutes of the Board of the Kentucky Christian Missionary Convention, there is information regarding what was paid to him when he represented the wider ministry of the church in serving small congregations in small mountain towns. In the minutes of the October Board meeting in 1899, it was recorded he had received two hundred fifty dollars for his work, presumably during that year. That is not to imply that sum was his entire income for the year. It does though reflect the difference in the amount of money ministers — or anyone for that matter — earned at a time which is more than a century ago. The level of income for clergy, then as now, was certainly below that of most other professions. Parenthetically, there are accounts in the records pertaining to the level of financial support the Board gave to those ministers who performed services on their behalf to the churches in various sections of the state. Since this story has to do with J.W. Masters, it seems appropriate to relate such information about his financial support from this Board. Masters made reports to H.W. Elliott, Secretary of the Board. He also kept other information — like sermon outlines, number of revivals, organizational meetings and the like (noted in the paragraph below). He kept these and other kinds of information in the small pocket-sized notebooks he carried. In the notebook he would often note the amount of money he received from the Kentucky State Board.

In addition to information about these various evangelists in the records of the Kentucky state organization, reports were also made to certain publications. In a 1900 issue of the *Christian Standard* publication, it stated in that same year, Masters' work extended over the entire section of Southeastern Kentucky. During March he was in the field seventeen days, baptized ten people, had one other addition. He reported these figures pertaining to the time and service he gave to one of the several churches in Whitley County. (There is an interesting note about the city of Corbin. The geography of the town is such that parts of the city are in three counties: Whitley, Knox, and Laurel. J.W. could be serving a couple of congregations in the same town, but in different counties.)

His August report to the State Board was similar to the one he made in March to the magazine: "At work seventeen days, added 38, aided one church, organized one church." Shelburne Masters remembered the West Corbin Christian Church to have been organized later, but the probable date was in 1900. Due to that section of Corbin being populated with a number of the Masters families, the locals then and now refer to the congregation simply as the Masterstown Church.

Two times I heard mention of what my great grandfather did in his spare time. Each time had to do with stories of fishing. One story came from my Uncle Shelburne.

> Our family moved from Laurel County [Keavy] back to Whitley County, where my father bought a farm. While we lived on the farm, my brothers and I tried to do the farm work. But when my father was home on Saturdays, he didn't care if we worked or not on the Saturdays he was home. He would take us down to the Laurel River and fish. When we'd work pretty good all week then he'd say, "Now, boys, I will take you fishing."

This story interests me because most of the time this man carried on his shoulders the weight of his struggling family. His shoulders also bore the weight of concern for several of the congregations where he had preached and ministered to the members. No doubt, he also felt the weight of the responsibility of his debates and the effect they had on his opponents and those in attendance. Yet in the midst of all that, occasionally, he found time for some relaxation and was able to go fishing with his boys. That was a bonding time and an overall good time.

His work the rest of that year was about the same as other years. A common task was his constant preaching for various county churches. Another task was raising money both for his family and the churches. Still another was the matter of locating preachers to serve the various congregations after he had completed his initiating or organizing work. In his Board report in 1900, Elliott gave high marks to his colleague Masters. He commended his work in the several churches where he had been preaching. In particular, Elliott was complementary about Masters' effectiveness in debating.

> Bro. Masters is regarded as a strong man in that region. Two houses of worship will soon be completed in Harlan County as the result of his efforts. He has located Bro. Osborne in that county, and the work will support him. This is a splendid piece of work. As a result of a debate held at Harlan Court House, recently, an entire congregation of another religious body, led by their preacher, accepted the Bible, and the Bible alone, as the only rule of faith and practice, and will henceforth be Christians only.

At the close of that year, J.W. made some changes in his work routine. He discontinued his work in Harlan County. Presumably, he brought to a close the time he devoted to preaching regularly for the State Board. This is a little difficult to understand, since Elliott, his friend and Secretary of the Board had commented about how effective he had been in his work in the region of Harlan. Masters reported from ten to twenty additions almost every month. Likely after securing J.K. Osborne to carry on the work in that territory he felt he could concentrate his efforts elsewhere. This seems to be the implication in the minutes of the Board, his employer.

The following appropriations were voted: $200 to aid J.K. Osborne in Harlan and adjoining counties — he to occupy the field formerly occupied by J.W. Masters, the latter having decided to change his field and not labor for this Board.

Tough Times All the Way Around

After years of personal friendship and professional association, to skip over without comment or review the matter of J.W. Masters leaving his relationship with the Kentucky State Board of Missions is too much of a skip. There is no hint in any of the material or information available that either mentions this move or suggests a reason for it happening. There is one thing throughout his long span of ministry that seems to be a constant in the life and work of this man of God. Always there was the underlying concern for his family's welfare and the need for money to provide for a large family. At about the turn of the century not many families in any of the mountain region had enough money to go around. Add to that the complexities and difficulties which were synonymous with evangelizing in the Southeastern Kentucky mountains and there always seemed to be a dilemma about where sufficient money was to come from to meet every day needs.

A comparison of "then and now' is both educational and revealing. A quick Google search revealed some general U.S. statistics for the year 1904. These statistics reveal how poor most families and communities were just over a hundred years ago. The figures reflect the economy of the whole country, not just Southeastern Kentucky.

- The average life expectancy in the U.S. was 47 years.
- Only 14% of the homes in the U.S. had a bathtub.
- The average wage was 22 cents per hour.
- The average worker made between $200 and $400 per year.
- 90% of all doctors had no college education. Instead, they attended so-called medical schools, many of which were condemned by the press and the government as *substandard*.
- Five leading causes of death in the U.S. were:
  1. Pneumonia and influenza
  2. Tuberculosis

3. Diarrhea
4. Heart disease
5. Stroke
- 2 out of every 10 adults could not read or write.
- Only 6% had graduated from high school.

To suggest the poor economy was a contributing factor to the standard of living for any family was true. J.W. Masters felt the pinch of the economy as keenly (and possibly more so) as anyone. Times were tough in the pre-World War I and pre-Great Depression days.

To search for some explanation for Masters to split from his work with the State Board is the same kind of exercise as the old "looking for a needle in a haystack." I intend neither to cast suspicion on my great grandfather's motives nor his ethics. It just may be that he thought he would be able to provide enough financial support for his family some other way — and thus not need to have the State Board continue to supplement him with funds that were needed by others who were also doing good work for the church.

Whatever the motive, the shift in his concentration of efforts was not a signal that J.W. Masters intended to slow down. His intentions were to continue to preach the gospel in the same manner in which he had devoted his exhaustive efforts for nearly forty years.

New and Old Ventures

In 1902 Masters concentrated a huge amount of his energies in Whitley and Laurel Counties. He also frequently journeyed elsewhere to hold revival meetings and answer the challenge of those hoping to gain an upper hand and best him at debating. As ready as he always was to preach the gospel, so was he ready to defend his faith in a debate. He held close to his heart the scripture, *"Always be ready to give a reason for the hope that lies in you." (1 Peter 3:15)* That summer he held a debate with a Seventh Day Adventist about the doctrine of the New Testament. The debate was conducted at Bush, Kentucky, near London.

To no one's surprise, his traveling schedule, preaching and debating meant Masters was gone most of the time from home. My Uncle Shelly remembered his father was home very few times on Sundays.

> There were very few Sundays in all my life that my father was ever home. Since I have been old enough to do so, I can't recall my father being home a single Sunday. We've been in meetings together in Harlan County, in Russell County, and in Alabama. But he was gone most of the time from home through the week and, as I say, always on Sundays.

My Aunt Lola remembered in the summer of 1902, her father baptized her and her older sister, Eunice. She said the baptism took place in a creek a short distance from Masterstown.

It was also in 1902, when the second debate between Masters and William Estes was held. Mr. Joseph Alsip, longtime resident of Corbin, told me that whereas the first debate between these two had been in London, this one was at Woodbine, outside Corbin. Again the issue of the debate was the doctrine of the church. My Aunt Eunice told me Mrs. Ada Gray Gilliam had told here about the Woodbine debate.

When they got off the train, Brother Estes shook hands with Brother Masters and said, "This is the man I am going to 'eat up' in this debate." But Mrs. Gilliam said that he did far from it. Although the debate was regarding the doctrine of the Christian Church, the part about which so much was said was on baptism. It was the consensus that my Daddy won the debate, and it was decided in his favor. This was done by the judges.

The mention of the role of judges is a reminder that having a debate on a given topic did not happen in a vacuum. There were guidelines and rules. There were the positions of moderator and judges to be appointed. There was the need for a location. Arrangements had to be made for chairs, fans, ushers and a "parking lot" for horses, buggies and wagons. There was PR to be done. There was the finalizing of a topic or subject for the debate which had to be approved ahead of time by both contenders. There was preparation, always preparation to be done. An event such as a debate had an equal number of components just as a Sunday morning worship service today. Today focus is upon the sanctuary and its ability to accommodate worshipers, and whether there is need for heat or AC. There are concerns for the choir, the organist and the competency of both. There is the need for hymnals, the comfort of the pews, a nursery and nursery keepers, deacons and elders to receive the offering and to administer communion. Worship and debates both require a lot of preparation.

A further thought regarding the comment about judges brings up another curious matter in debates between differing religious viewpoints. One cannot overlook the matter of "ground rules." Each contender had an allotted amount of time in each of a predetermined number of presentations. Each contender was allowed to make comments uninterrupted. Following each speech, each contender was allowed time for rebuttal. That was followed by points or remarks in a counter-rebuttal. As a general rule, usually there were an odd number of judges. Presumably, the judges were agreed upon by both contenders. The outcome of the debate was determined by the judges.

Before we stray too far from the subject of baptism, as mentioned in the previous story, about this time Masters told of hearing an old Primitive Baptist preacher give a testimonial. The Primitive Baptist gave a definition of "baptism" without using a dictionary.

The old preacher, once of the mountains, had a regular monthly appointment near where I was holding a meeting. I went to hear him. In his sermon, he told his religious experience. He began:

"When I started to get religious I went up on the mountain to pray, and it seemed that I was doing no good, so I quit, started back down the mountain, and some kind of a power pressed me to my knees, and in a few minutes Jesus came into my soul. Then I started home, shouting as I went. The thought came to me that I must be baptized next. But how? Some say sprinkling, some say pouring, some say immersion. I then fell to my knees again, and asked that power to tell me how to be baptized.

"The power lifted me to my feet and sent me down the mountain whirling. At the foot of the mountain was a pond of water; I was going toward it. I tried to go to the left, but could not; then to the right, and could not. And I tell you, brethren, that I was going in a fast gait. And right at the edge of the pond I stumped my toe, and into the pond I went head and ears.

"This showed me how to be baptized. But, brethren, at that time I had but little Bible sense.

Had I known then what I do now, I could have solved the problem. Here it is: When I baptize a man his back hits the water, bap, and I raise him up; the water streams from his clothes, tism; put the two (bap and tism) together and you have baptism."

The old fellow fixed it about right... sprinkling has neither *bap* nor *tism*.

This kind of story might raise eyebrows and bring frowns, but to certain individuals like the old Primitive Baptist preacher from the mountains, this sort of uneducated logic made sense.

In the first part of 1903, Masters received his call to conduct another revival at the Whetstone Christian Church. During this meeting he baptized the three youngest daughters of Judge Stinson of Williamsburg. The Stinsons, who had moved into Williamsburg from out in the county, often visited the "old home church." A fourth and older daughter, Lila, was present during this revival. Lila Stinson and her sisters were second cousins to Dave Stinson whom I have mentioned frequently. It was at this revival that she first met John W. Masters. Lila was in her early twenties at the time of the revival. In her late years, I visited Mrs. Lila Stinson. During the interview, her recollection of the revival was still sharp. She thought highly of "Mr. Masters" as a preacher.

Having terminated his work with the State Board of Missions a couple of years previously, J.W. continued to live in Corbin for a year and a half following the close of his Harlan ministry. Surmising about why he concluded his present work with the State Board, the question remains as to whether or not something different might open for him. Indeed, it was not long before a new field of endeavor beckoned, and Masters responded.

I mentioned early on that in one of Masters' humble attempts at preaching in his home country of Southwestern Virginia, he met Dr. Joseph Hopwood, President of Milligan College, Tennessee. Although at the outset, Dr. Hopwood was far from being impressed with Masters' capabilities as a public speaker.

In time and with the awareness of Masters maturing, he grew to admire and respect the one time awkward but totally sincere preacher. They became lasting friends. In the spring of 1903 Joseph Hopwood went to Lynchburg, Virginia, as President of Lynchburg College. Either by correspondence or in person he asked the now mature Masters to take the Vice Presidency of Milligan College.[23] The invitation obviously meant that he would live there. Masters accepted the invitation to go to Milligan and live but declined the invitation to become Vice President. He may have felt the offer was based upon friendship rather than his experience and expertise in academic matters. Such an administrative position was out of his range of competency. In any role he had held previously in his earlier academic pursuits, it had been without experience in any instructional position. He accepted the invitation but declined the position.

---

[23] This information is based on two sources: [1] It came from my Aunt Eunice Young, his daughter who was a young teen at the time. [2] There was also a report in the *Christian Standard* of a change of location for the Masters family in making a move from Corbin to Milligan in 1903. Thus, due to his strong feelings for and admiration of J.W. Masters, my aunt reported Dr. Hopwood extended an invitation to her father to come to the Milligan campus. We need not presume, however, the invitation to come to the college to have been for a position involving his presence in the classroom for instructional purposes. According to several references — as we will see later — the probability is the Presidentt of the college wanted Masters' presence on the campus and in the chapel, perhaps even to do fund raising.

Days at Milligan College

According to the July 1903 edition of the *Christian Standard*, J.W. Masters made a move from Corbin, Ky., to Milligan, Tenn. Following the move to Tennessee, Masters soon returned to his native Virginia to conduct a revival meeting in Appalachia, in Wise County. His oldest daughter, Sallie, had not long before married John O. Blondell, who had been born and reared in Appalachia, Virginia. As a result of this revival my great grandfather was instrumental in converting and then baptizing his new son-in-law, my grandfather.

During the next few years the trail of this mountain preacher wound through Eastern Tennessee and Southwestern Virginia, where he often preached and occasionally debated. One such debate was in Pennington Gap, Virginia. In his book, *Sketches of the Pioneers*, J.W. West mentions this debate.

> The writer of this sketch loaned [Masters] a tent in which to hold a debate at Pennington Gap, Virginia, with Prof. Hurst, a Primitive Baptist. I heard the debate. So able was [Masters] in establishing the time when the Church of Christ was established that Prof. Hurst endorsed his argument.

Given his reputation as an historian, I regard the foregoing statement by West to be quite commendable. Masters also made reference to this particular debate.

> I was called back in my old home district in Virginia to debate with a Primitive Baptist who was a professor in one of the schools, and I believe he was the most honest man I ever debated with. The third day of the debate I made an argument on the establishment of the church. Of course, I showed that the church was built on the day of Pentecost and not in the days of John the Baptist,

and, to my surprise, my opponent endorsed it. He said, "Brother Masters has given the truth on the subject, and I can not afford to deny it," and took his seat, waiting for my next speech. After the debate he said to Dr. Shelburne: "I acknowledge my defeat." Our people were expecting him to identify himself with us, but he was accidentally killed a few days afterward.[24]

During the time he lived at Milligan, J.W. preached occasionally at the church on the Milligan campus. Part of the flexibility of his position when he accepted the invitation/challenge to go to the college was preaching for the student body. The chapel building was in a prior chapel to the one now standing. I was in the Hopwood Memorial Building when I attended church youth camp there as a teenager. My Uncle Shelly informed me that "lots of mornings my father preached at the chapel sessions for the students of Milligan College." The initial chapel was probably replaced with the Hopwood Memorial Building, constructed a good many years later.

In attempting to follow the trail of this mountain preacher (as the title of his own book states) it is not difficult to realize that J.W. Masters was a restless soul. He could not be in all the places he wanted to be at the same time. His moves and his alliances were many. Such restlessness invites speculation. Perhaps due to this restlessness, he had a constant desire and willingness to be on the move in order to answer any and every call to those desiring his services. Could it be every voice he heard from the trails he felt to be the voice of God? Could it be this inner feeling was again a sort of struggle, similar to that earlier time when he made frequent changes in locations and/or employment? Could it be he had a need to equal or surpass the admiration and respect he had for his father and mentor in ministry in order to gain his or other's approval? Could it have been his competitive spirit which showed through in each and every debate he held? Could it be learning to fight in the battle of overcoming his stuttering

---

24   The statement by Professor Hurst to Dr. Shelburne may or may not indicate that Shelburne was one of the judges for the debate.

in earlier years now translated into this competitive spirit which now was present in nearly all of his speaking? Could it be this is how he felt he must perform as a father to his young and maturing family? Could it be this is how he defined himself as a minister proclaiming the Word of God? Could it be this was the way he defined his sense of response to The Call to Ministry?

Something was moving this spiritual titan. His pioneering spirit was always beckoning J.W. Masters into ever different and newer circles of service for his Lord. A man of contentment he was not. Some such matter always seemed to be pushing him onward and motivating him in new directions, new challenges and even new enterprises.

A few times during this period, his reports "from the field" were made in both the *Christian Evangelist* and the *Christian Standard* publications. Seeing as how in time these two magazines came to represent different elements within the Stone-Campbell movement, J.W. Masters undoubtedly made reports in both in order to reach a broader readership and show the extent of his work in the mountain counties of Kentucky.

This both/and reporting style was prior to the signs of disunity beginning to spread among the congregations in the Stone-Campbell movement. Eventually, the two magazines became extensions of the differing theological positions resident throughout the movement in the late 19th century and beginning of the 20th. Any full time evangelist such as J.W. Masters needed to reach the widest audience possible. Invitations for revivals and invitations to otherwise preach were welcomed from any source. If the chance to spread the word about his availability for such services to the church could be increased by utilizing more than one instrument of publication, that represented one more opportunity for J.W. Masters to preach and work in more fields.

In spite of his official relationship with (or apart from) the State Board of Kentucky, Masters continued to make regular reports for his time and energy in his preaching. The following is a sample of the way his reports were listed month after month. In the early part of 1903, he reported on his work in East Tennessee.

- "Milligan, December 24 — Preached four weeks at Mt. Carmel and Liberty, Johnson County, with 40 additions — 36 baptisms. J.W. Masters."
- "Milligan, February 11, Just closed a meeting at Hales Chapel"[25] with 32 additions — 27 baptisms. J.W. Masters."
- "Milligan, March 21, — Twelve additions since last report. Success to the Standard. J.W. Masters."
- "Milligan, April 18, — Twenty-two additions at Hampton. The Bible-alone plea is gaining ground. J.W. Masters."
- "Milligan, May 25 — Just closed a meeting at Boones Creek, with 19 additions. I baptized a woman ninety-two years old. She had never been a member of any church and had not been in a church house for thirty years. J.W. Masters."
- "Milligan, June 18, — Thirteen additions since last report. The truth properly presented wins. God stands at the back of it. J.W. Masters."

In his May report, Masters mentioned a meeting at Boones Creek. This church is just outside Jonesboro, Tennessee. He preached there several times while his family was living at Milligan. Additionally he was called back to Boones Creek for revivals after he moved from the area.

Very little information is available regarding Masters' production over the next couple of years. I did learn, however, from my Uncle Shelburne that his father had two debates during a sojourn in Tennessee. Both were with the same man, a Mr. E.D. Cox in the eastern part of Tennessee.

The first one with Cox was in Shady Valley, Tennessee, just outside Elizabethton. This was about 1904 or 1905. We lived at Milligan in 1903

---

[25] During the greater part of my college years at Johnson Bible College, I was pastor of a small congregation in Clinchport, Virginia. Clinchport is no more than 30 or 40 miles from Milligan College. At the time I was familiar with this territory and several churches, such as Hales Chapel. I found in my initial research, that the 1962 Yearbook of the Christian Church (Disciples of Christ) still listed a Hales Chapel in Washington County, Virginia.

and 1904. And I think that the other one was at Thorn Grove, Tennessee. That is where the Baptist preacher lived. He went back down there boasting what he had done. [Thorn Grove is in Knox County not far from Johnson Bible College.] And so they wrote for my father. [Mr. Cox] said that he made my father slip clear across the mourner's bench. And that just got my father, and he took off and said "I will make him think 'swing and slip' when I get through with him a second time." And they had it.

Evidently, Masters *was* "out to get him" the second time for he relates a brief part of the second debate in his book.

Soon after... I had two [debates] in Tennessee with the same man — E.D. Cox. The second one was held in a brick building in the month of December, a rainy day. The windows were crowded [with folks looking in] from the outside, making the room rather dark. My opponent was trying to read, and said to me: "Brother Masters, I need light." "Yes, I see you do and I will give you some when I take the floor," I answered.

A Perchance Visit to Johnson Bible College

In 1905, Masters received a request to preach in Knoxville. This request came from his friend Mr. Jones who, years before, had moved from Corbin, Kentucky, to Rogersville, Tennessee. At the time of this invitation Mr. Jones lived in Knoxville. J.W. went to Knoxville and preached, at least on one occasion, in the Forest Avenue Christian Church.[26]

It was of particular interest to me to learn that some time during these years in his travels in the Knoxville and Thorn Grove area, my Grandpa Masters made the acquaintance of Ashley S. Johnson, founder of Johnson Bible College, Kimberlin Heights, Tennessee. I could not determine, however, whether my great grandfather was ever on the campus of that school. The thought of an encounter with Ashley Johnson has raised the level of my curiosity. As I said, did he make it to the campus? Did his visit with Dr. Johnson serve a similar purpose of an interview as did the one issued by Dr. Hopwood? Did he preach in a chapel service in Old Main, most probably the only building in existence at the time? There is a lingering and haunting nostalgic question for me. Would it not be an act of providence if a visit to the campus of Johnson Bible College was one more way that the paths of my great grandfather and me have crossed?

Speaking of nostalgia, approximately at the time of his East Tennessee ministry, J.W. Masters preached in the community of Clinchport, Virginia, near his boyhood home in Scott County. Before the present Clinchport congregation was organized, there was a Union Church at a location near Natural Tunnel, Virginia. The Union Church site is where he preached. Natural Tunnel

---

[26]   I mention two items here. [1] Interestingly enough, years later a granddaughter of J.W. Masters and her family were members of the Forest Avenue congregation. Mrs. Aileen (Foster) Setser, daughter of Mrs. Eunice Young, was that grand-daughter. [2] Additionally, a 1957 graduate and classmate of my mine from Johnson Bible College, Dr. David L. Eubanks — immediate Past President of Johnson Bible College held that position for 39 years. For a number of years he served as the minister of that fine Knoxville congregation.

and Clinchport are neighboring communities, only a few miles apart.

I have always been curious to know whether or not Rebecca Masters (J.W.'s first wife) ever accompanied her husband on his trips into Scott County. I simply mention this again because it was also the home territory of Mrs. Masters, whose maiden name, of course, was Robinett. While I was student Pastor at the Clinchport congregation, there was a Robinett family which was well respected throughout the community. At the time, some members of the family were active participants in the Clinchport congregation. When they learned of my kinship to J.W. Masters, some of the old timers in that area spoke admirably to me of Brother Masters. Thereafter, members of the Robinett family and I often spoke of being kin folks.

From the time J.W. Masters made his first horseback journey into Kentucky in the mid-1880s, he developed a strong bond and attachment for the people there. That bond was especially true for the folks in Southeastern Kentucky. Over this nearly 20 year period, there were many signs of growth in this man and his concept of what it would take for him to proclaim the gospel and promote the Kingdom of God.

Masters experienced growth in his association with the common folks among the mountain people. He grew in his affiliation with the leaders in the work of the Kentucky State Board of Missions. He grew in his willingness to discipline himself in documenting his expanding work as the evangelist he was. He grew in his determination to give significant time and energy to the best of his ability to promote the "Plea" — the use of the Bible alone — of the Stone-Campbell cause, known also as the Restoration Movement. This is especially true in the signs of his growth as a strong preacher. There was no longer funny or joking remarks directed at this man's command of the English language or his ability to proclaim his faith in Jesus Christ as Lord.

Perhaps as much as anything else, the ministry of this Masters during these years took on a greater sense of accomplishment due to his maturing ability to communicate to the audiences to whom he proclaimed his simple yet profound message. The key factor in that development was the shift from one who stood in the pulpit stammering and stuttering (making his listeners both embarrassed and apologetic for him and his efforts at preaching) and virtually stumping his toes every time he got up to speak. He obviously moved to the other end of the spectrum as an eloquent preacher who stood tall in the pulpit while he clearly, without obstruction convincingly and unashamedly presented an articulate message of the Bible to those eager to hear and willing to receive that message. He became the confident and accomplished evangelist he hoped to be. The youthful would-be cleric who stood in the woods preaching to the tree-stumps had now advanced himself and the cause of the Kingdom. He now stood in pulpits and chapels across a whole region with vigor and zeal eloquently delivering his message of the gospel. He preached both to the farming community who wore overalls and straw hats as well as to the business community and those wearing academic caps and gowns. It was during the time while he was in the throes of decision regarding the kind of career he should choose that he discovered his real/only love: ministry. Thus, having decided he could not practice law, he was glad he decided to preach... and never from that point on had trouble speaking. "Before I had time to begin the study of law I came to the conclusion that I could not succeed both as a lawyer and a preacher, so I gave the law idea up... bless your soul, I don't have to carry a bullet in my mouth now. I can talk without it." The efforts of this mountain pioneer preacher fused together his passion and zeal for the burden on his soul. All he ever wanted to do was to preach the gospel to all within the sound of his voice.

Like many a modern minister who makes frequent moves from one church to another, after only a few years in his Tennessee ministry (including his journeys into neighboring communities in Virginia), the restless spirit of J.W. Masters was again giving voice to his enthusiasm and a tug on his desire for a return to a place of familiarity. He yearned for his home in Kentucky. There he had made friends; there lived his kinsmen; there he had bought and sold land; there he had given of himself in countless hours toward the work of the Kingdom of God; there he had preached and baptized; there he had organized congregations and watched them grow and flourish. There were the people of the mountains of Southeastern Kentucky whom he loved.

He longed to go back; and go back he did.

YEARS OF MATURITY

What Goes Around Comes Around

In early 1906, the John W. Masters family moved from Tennessee back to Kentucky. Their whole extended family welcomed J.W. and his family back to their Kentucky home. From this time forward, no member of the entire Masters family ever lived for any extended period of time outside Kentucky.

Soon after this return J.W. contacted H.W. Elliott, who was still Secretary of the Kentucky Board of Missions. He requested to be employed to preach and again represent the State Board. At the February meeting of the Board, approval was granted and this minister to the mountains was again authorized to work on behalf of the Board of Missions. His first assignment was with the Wallin's Creek congregation in Harlan County. Concurrently, he preached on several occasions in Jackson, Laurel, and Clay Counties. When it was time for him to be "back in the saddle," he saddled up his horse and was back in business. J.W.'s pattern of reporting was taken up where he left off: he reported his activities among the churches to the Missions Board, and also relayed the information to be published in the *Christian Standard*. It was not uncommon for J.W. to report from one to three or four dozen additions per month. A typical report was in the May edition of the *Christian Standard*.

J.W. Masters was at work 27 days in Whitley and Laurel counties. 35 additions; one Sunday School, one prayer meeting and one congregation constituted. A visit was made to Legal, Ky., and plans perfected for building a house of worship.

When my father-in-law, J.B. Johnson, Sr., was but a young boy, he heard John Masters preach at Whetstone Christian Church. He wrote of his boyhood impressions.

> I heard John W. Masters preach at Whetstone more than once. Granddaddy Sharp took me; I rode behind him on a horse. We then lived about four miles away. Of course I was very young. I would say between six and twelve, because I was twelve when Granddaddy died.

> My memory is that Brother Masters was a sturdy, but not stout man in personal appearance. I am sure that he had a mustache, and wore a white collar (perhaps celluloid; they were in vogue in those days). He rode very erect, on a good looking dark bay or black horse.

> I can't say that I remember anything he said in his sermons. I do remember, vividly, that he had pulpit vitality and emphasis. I also recall that on one of the occasions as we traveled home, preacher Gunny Hill and Granddaddy Sharp talked about how his sermon was as "plain as the nose on your face." As they expressed it, he had been able to cinch his argument on the *meaning of the Scriptures*. I remember this because it was the first time I had ever heard the expression, "plain as the nose on your face."

Earlier I mentioned Andrew Walker, a prominent citizen and editor of the Corbin Daily Tribune in those days. He also held a position of professor of education in the Corbin system. In the spring of 1906, Mr. Walker bought a farm adjoining the one owned by Masters in West Corbin. The two became acquainted and subsequently, good friends. They had many conversations and many pleasant experiences. In addition to his comments on a debate which I have mentioned earlier, he also talked about his personal relationship with my great grandfather. Mr. Walker's memory was still sharp. He relayed several stories and pieces of information. Apparently he was quite younger than my great grandfather. His recollections were very favorable.

> Brother Masters never did speak unkindly of individuals, but he did of their doctrines. He was a big individual. He had great conviction. This was shown in many ways. I considered them a model family in the community. They were the nicest neighbors. Eunice, Masters' daughter, often stayed with Mrs. Walker when I would be away from home for overnight trips.

On one occasion Mr. Walker told me Brother Masters lent him two books to read. They were biographical works pertaining to "two men of the Christian Church brotherhood." He remembered one book about a preacher known as "Raccoon" John Smith. (Every church historian is familiar with the name of "Raccoon" John Smith. But for those who haven't heard of him, he was an ardent spokesman, and capable representative for the followers of Alexander Campbell.) Mr. Walker said after he read the books, he and Masters discussed them at length. Walker told me he was not of the same religious persuasion as his neighbor and friend. He was quite aware that the able persuader had hopes of wining him over to his side. But Walker remained a Baptist and never did become convinced of Masters' position on theology. Even though they did not see eye-to-eye on religious matters, they remained close friends. Mr. Walker told me in spite of their differences, "Brother Masters always treated me as a Christian brother."

The only time there could have been hard feelings between Masters and his good neighbor occurred about a year after Walker had moved to his new farm. He was asked to teach in the Masterstown school. Masters was neither on the School Board nor did he have any connection with the school regarding hiring teachers. Yet, he disapproved of the appointment of Mr. Walker as teacher there. Walker said it was because he was not a member of the Christian Church. If this accusation was true, there was never a hint in any other incident where this sort of vindictive behavior on the part of John W. Masters ever surfaced. Truth be told, he may have had reasons or personal feelings for his opposition to Walker as a teacher of which he never spoke. Even in light of this particular insight, it can still be said that J.W. Masters always held to his beliefs, even if it caused a breach in friendship. In any event, Mr. Walker was kind in his remarks regarding this incident.

> Rev. Masters, naturally, had a lot of influence in the community and, thus, they didn't hire me as the teacher of the school. But at the same time I received a call to come to Knox County and teach; so I left the Masterstown community, accepting the invitation to go to Knox County, and therefore made no issue of the matter. I considered Masters a man "fixed in his doctrine."

When asked about some of the sideline interests of his neighbor, John Masters, Mr. Walker referred to what he called J.W.'s interest in *progressive* farming. That is, he was speaking of *scientific* farming. He said "your [great] grandfather Masters put lime on his field at the proper time of the year, turned the soil, and applied any other method that was being promoted to better develop farming." Quite simply, this indicates that J.W. Masters was interested in and willing to use whatever "new" or "innovative" element he could to make improvements — whether it be in religion or farming or whatever.

Ganging Up for A Fight

According to his schedule, the first six months of 1906 had already been a busy time for J.W. Masters. Along with his heavy preaching schedule, a report in the *Christian Standard* said he conducted a revival at the Wallin's Creek Church in May which provided an unusual experience. He began the revival in Harlan County and was met at the first service by five Baptist ministers who challenged him to a debate. To most preachers a challenge of that magnitude from a team of five preachers would prove too formidable. But such was not the case with John Masters. On the spot, he immediately let them know of his intentions to accommodate them and accepted the challenge. The *Christian Standard* said that he debated four days with J.G. Parsons at Wallin's Creek. Using the rich dialogue between them, I quote the entire passage Masters wrote about this debate.

> Five Baptist preachers met me at an appointment on one of the creeks, and presented a written challenge for a debate. I told them that I was not seeking a debate, but, if they would put up a representative, that they were barking up the right kind of a tree to get all they wanted. They said they had the man. We set the time and the place for the debate. They sent to another part of the State for their man. The man came two or three days before time. The day before the debate began, a friend told me that the new man had told that I was once a member of the Baptist Church. I told my friend we would have fun in the morning just before the

debate begins. So the next morning[27] we had a large crowd. I called the attention of my opponent and told him what was going the rounds. He denied saying it. I said my informant is in the house, who will speak for himself. [Pointing to one of the ministers] he arose, saying: "That Baptist preacher sitting yonder told me." [The Baptist preacher he pointed to] said: "I heard him say it." "Oh," said my opponent, "Brother Masters, I told them that I had understood that you were a member of the Baptist Church when you were a boy." "All right," I said; "if I was, you voted me in while I was asleep and voted me out before I awoke." We then went to work, all in a good humor.

My opponent got into the pulpit to prove that the Baptist Church is Scriptural, and he read Daniel 2:44, then jumped to Matthew 16:18. From this he went into his bosom and brought out a little book, opened it, laid it on his Bible, and began reading about the Baptist Church. When he closed his speech, I took the floor, saying: "Your jump from Daniel 2:44 to Matthew 16:18 I think was a wise jump, but what about the next jump — when you brought out the little book from your bosom? Why did you go into your bosom? Why did you not continue to read your Bible? Of course I knew, and all these Baptist preachers knew, the reason. You wanted to read about the Baptist Church, and you

---

[27] The reference here to a morning service has occurred before, but a comment here is in order. Frequently when there were debates or preaching services, there is mention they took place "in the morning." As always there were services on Sunday mornings, but this had to do with debates. So whether they took place in the morning or at night, folks made time in their schedule to attend. In our time, however, that kind of thing couldn't very easily happen. Work, school teaching, interest in television programs and other matters would certainly compete with and perhaps prevent such gatherings any time during the day nowadays.

could not do it in the Bible and had to get the book from your bosom." Just then he said: "I can read about the Baptist Church in the Bible." I replied: "Will you do it in your next speech?" "Yes," he said. Then I addressed the audience, saying that he would not mention it in his next speech. Sure enough, he never referred to it. I asked him why he did not mention it. He said; "My time expired before I could get to it." Then I said: "If you had time, would you make an effort?" He said "Yes." Then I said, "The next half-hour is mine; take it," and sat down. Poor fellow! I got sorry for him. He reminded me of a young man who went a-courting one night, and his girl went to bed and left him sitting. He said: "I wish I was to home." The debate lasted four days, and ended by my friends presenting me with a beautiful bouquet with a new twenty-dollar bill pinned to it. This all happened in old Harlan County, where some of the best people in the world live.

The above story contains rugged comments and a straight-forwardness not present in many church meetings toady. The tone of this story reminds me of statements Mr. Joe Alsip made to me. Mr. Alsip was an educator in the public school system and one of the old-timers in Whitley County. (At the time we talked, Mr. Alsip lived in Corbin. Later on, he moved to Lexington and our friendship has continued.) "I can tell you one thing about old Brother Masters," Mr. Alsip said. "He was the ablest preacher in the mountains of Kentucky. He could say the hardest things and nobody would get mad. He'd always come around in the nicest way. Yesiree, he stayed right with it. He had a way of always bringing out the funny thing in a situation and nobody could get mad at what he said." Again and again, his penchant for humor surfaced in his dealings with folks.

Secretary Elliott said Masters worked in Leslie County during July; conducted a revival and had 23 additions. He had a strong desire to go to the remote County-seat town of Hyden for a revival in October.

In addition to his preaching responsibilities in Eastern Kentucky, Masters was always thinking about the overall cultural, spiritual and educational needs of those to whom he preached. He enhanced the work of the churches in that region. Elliott commented on his work. "J.W. Masters has been laying siege to Harlan Court House. He has gathered together 18 people there, had a lot and some money given without getting help outside of the county. He regards that place a fine opening for a school and thinks that our people could do much for that region by establishing one."[28]

---

[28] Very likely, J.W. Masters regarded the role of public education with nearly the same amount of importance he gave to the matter of religious education. One must remember how diligently he worked for the establishment of a college in Corbin in the late 1890s. This kind of encouragement for the role of education in society has always been consistent with other leaders and the denomination of the Christian Church (Disciples of Christ) in general. One simply needs to think of the emphasis Alexander Campbell placed on the need for quality education. Thus, it was consistent for Masters likewise to be concerned for the need for education in general.

David N. Blondell

Providing Support Meant Total Commitment

Riding horseback, J.W. Masters travelled from one county to another preaching in schools, court houses, and churches — anywhere he could to gain an audience for the opportunity to proclaim the gospel. He spent 23 days in Clay County in August in a revival and again had 23 additions. H.W. Elliott reported the results: "Masters appointed six officers and constituted a congregation." One source said this new church was in Fogertown, Ky. The official record, however, places the beginning of the Fogertown congregation a dozen years later.

Masters reported that the "house" at Harlan was progressing well. As a result of his success in Harlan, he made contacts with folks from neighboring areas and hence, conducted revivals beyond the region of Harlan. In September of that year, he spent time in a community on the Bell and Harlan County line. He baptized a couple dozen folks "in a community where we have never been heard until now. A number of heads of families were added, and we are assured of an organization and the building of a house of worship. This will be our first house in Bell County outside of Pineville and Middlesboro."

Establishing new churches was one of John Masters' strengths. He was convincing in his ability to demonstrate the basic, biblical components of a church. He knew how St. Paul in his letters to the churches spoke about their organizational structure. His charisma enabled him to succeed in these efforts in the spirit of the Apostle. The task of pinpointing the churches that were reportedly established by him, however, is one which is difficult at best and sometimes almost impossible. Secretary Elliott reported in the *Christian Evangelist* the following year regarding Master's work in the Bell and Harlan County region. A congregation known as the Church at Puckett's Creek was started there.

J.W. Masters ended his busy year of 1906
still working in Harlan and Bell Counties. At the

November meeting of the State Board, the record indicated that during the next year he was to continue devoting time in Middlesboro, but also extending into other portions of Bell County. Added to that were the names of Harlan, Perry, Leslie and Knott Counties.

Early in 1907, Masters was invited to return to Whetstone Church in Whitley County and conduct a revival. (In a conversation I had with Mr. Doc Sullivan, he mentioned Brother Masters preaching at a Whetstone anniversary service that year. The records of the church show it was at a later date. This revival meeting lasted for several weeks. As usual, there were many additions.

There is an amazing item in his report to the *Christian Standard,* which followed that revival. The statement said J.W. Masters had *"preached 55 sermons"* in the month of January in 1907. To begin with, that was at a time when this man was about fifty-three years of age! Any minister, at any age, can easily recognize the enormity of such a task as preaching *fifty-five* sermons in any one month period of time. It helps to understand this preaching schedule came at the height of his career. It also helps to realize this man lived in one community and rode horseback to several other communities outside that community to fulfill preaching appointments.

The task becomes more complex when we realize his heavy preaching docket was also in the winter season when traveling in the mountains of Southeastern Kentucky was a lot more difficult and sometimes a great deal more treacherous than it is today, or at other seasons in the year. Complete that scenario by realizing the preaching was done in the single month of January in the mountains, and it makes this astonishing feat virtually unbelievable. Especially, I need to say, I have never known of a single individual who could stand up to the almost impossible riggers of that preaching schedule at virtually any age!

A Unique Debate Tactic

Mr. Joe Alsip told me it was approximately during this time that Masters held a debate with Simmy Holt, a Baptist preacher, at Mauney's Chapel in Whitley County. "One little thing happened in that debate," Mr. Alsip said casually. "Holt's moderator came into the Christian Church." The issue during the debate dealt with the doctrine of the two churches. One realizes what an impact it must have been at the time of the debate and in the community to have that kind of thing happen. At the conclusion of the debate, the moderator of one side joins forces with those of the other! How's that for intense and high drama!

Speaking of Grandpa's debates, I have a boyhood recollection of a story of one of his debates. I heard about this debate both from my father and my great uncle Shelburne. I have no idea as to the presumed date or location. While I cannot attest fully to its authenticity, I heard the two of them mention it on more than one occasion. It is the most memorable story I ever heard Uncle Shelburne tell about any debate his father had.

The occasion was between Grandpa and his opponent regarding the topic of Predestination, a frequent subject of debates in those days. The gentleman speaking in the affirmative position was the first to address the audience. Prior to beginning his remarks in the speaking rotation, the man had taken time to place in the middle of the platform a small wooden stand. He placed on the stand a shiny red apple. His complete argument focused on the apple. He said it was conceived by the Almighty in the beginning of the foundation of the world. It had retained that same design throughout history. It had not evolved in design as had other elements of creation. There was absolutely nothing that either he or his "worthy opponent" could do to change or alter this object of creation.

He went on, ad nauseam, with his attempt to prove since the beginning of time, every apple has been the result of a seed being planted, a tree developing into maturity, growth occurring and the end result being the product such as "this bright shiny apple sitting on the stand behind me." He emphasized that the apple on the stand had accomplished this process with neither interference nor assistance from any outside source. He closed his argument stating that no thing or no person could prevent the apple from being the "beautiful red fruit" it was predestined to be. He said it was the most obvious example of the doctrine of Predestination. At that point he turned to pick up the apple.

Unknown to the speaker — who was paying closer attention to his audience as he made point after convincing point, than he was to his fellow debater — something took place on the platform of which he was not aware. Several minutes into the debate Mr. Masters had reached over from his seated position, picked up the apple and began taking bites out of it. By the time the gentleman turned around to pick up the apple to prove to his audience the brilliance of his remarks, all that was left was the core. The audience found this to be enlightening and not a little amusing. Masters never spoke. The proponent of Predestination left the platform, also without speaking again. The *debate* was over. The folks all went home. End of story.

Events Here and There

In April and May of 1907, Masters worked in Bell and Harlan Counties raising $380 to build a house of worship. The building was for the congregation established the previous fall on Puckett's Creek, in Bell County. My Aunt Eunice Young told me about it.

> During the time he was concentrating his attention in Bell County my Dad attended a revival in Middlesboro which was being conducted by a Brother Owsley. During the course of the evening, there was to be a baptismal ceremony. There was a young boy to be sprinkled; this was a church which did not practice immersion. At the time of the sprinkling, the child ran out. And Brother Owsley looked over at my Dad and said, "Brother Masters, what would you do if that were you?" And he replied, "Well, if I did that like you do it, I'd bring me a squirt-gun." (The two of them were the very best of friends. My Dad could always say what he wanted to but he never made any enemies.)

The nature of an evangelist is to evangelize. Thus, occasions were rare when Masters was not out of town preaching. When he was home and the opportunity afforded itself, he loved to go fishing. Dave Stinson said one hot summer day Brother Masters was down in the river fishing in a *flat bottom* boat.[29] Some boys came along and decided they would pull a prank on him. One of the boys got a large lard can and turned it upside down over his head and got into the water. All that could be seen above the water was the can. The boy approached Masters in the boat. When Masters saw the mysterious object coming toward him in the water, he got the boat to the bank as quickly as possible and

---

[29] The term "flat bottom" was a common term indicating such a boat was most likely home-made.

deserted it, exclaiming, "Brother, if you want it that bad, I will just leave it with you."

My Uncle Jasper (W.J. Young), son-in-law of J.W. Masters and husband of Eunice, told me of a revival held by his father-in-law in a schoolhouse not far from Roger's Ford — either in Knox County or Whitley County. I was unable to pinpoint the precise time of this revival, but according to the content it must have been during cold weather. Mr. Bunch was a friend of Uncle Jasper and told him about an incident which occurred while he attended the revival. Uncle Jasper shared the following story.

> Mr. Bunch wore a heavy beard nearly all the time. In this particular revival, the weather turned very cold. Bunch had on an overcoat when he entered the building. Brother Masters was preaching. In addition to the overcoat, the old man Bunch had a shawl tied over his hat and under his chin. Of course, that *bush* he was behind made him look terrible. When he entered the building, my daddy-in-law just stopped long enough to say to someone sitting in front, "Now, Brother So-and-So, if anything comes in this building from here on out that looks any worse than this follow does," and pointing to a window behind the pulpit, "I will jump out this window." Well, there was an old man by the name of Whitman — and he was sort of a frightful sight to look at. He always wore a heavy beard, and wasn't very clean at that. He rode a big, old mule. He often came by our old home place. He was a funny looking sort of character. Just about the time Brother Masters got started real good again (as Bunch remembered) Whitman came in. The fellow Masters had spoken

to earlier was sitting near the front. He said, "Brother Masters, bust 'er!"[30]

From the interviews I conducted, I gained significant information about a basic approach used by Brother Masters. I asked most of the people what they thought to be the most outstanding characteristic of J.W. Masters. The majority said it was his ability to find humor in a situation and express it without being offensive. Such statements have convinced me of the genuine sense of humor this mountaineer preached possessed. Such a characteristic made him unique.

---

[30] My Uncle Jasper told me Grandpa Masters "could get through one of those things — a thing like that — in a sermon, and could go right on without missing a single thought. He could just go from a joke into something serious or from something serious into a joke. I have heard that out at the old home church plenty of times. And for which, he was criticized. They said he told too many jokes."

Working with Congregations...
Attending to Family Matters

Toward the end of 1907, Secretary Elliott gave his November report to the Board of Missions. He reported that Masters had organized a new congregation. His only comment was, "This makes four in Harlan County, where a few years ago we had nothing." Period! That is it! Nothing more. In spite of the often lengthy reports Mr. Elliott gave in regard to the district evangelists, I was disappointed and disturbed when I read this brief statement.

It was not just the matter of not giving more accolades to my great grandfather. When one is assessing the value of such a tireless laborer as John W. Masters, I thought surely, stating the man had established four new churches in one county deserved some comment more than what he made. The report makes no mention of a specific church: its name, its location, any of the members. Nothing! From what Mr. Elliott reported, it cannot be determined anything about the one church or who or where the other churches were or anything about them. One can only surmise the locations or names in such reports. His viewpoint seems to parallel that of my Grandpa: stating specific facts such as individual names and places was not of singular importance. The fact that a great work for the Lord was being accomplished there where nothing was happening previously was the point! Put in that context, I withdraw my comment and conclude such a viewpoint is good enough for me.

When J.W. Masters moved his family to Corbin in the early 1890's, his father and mother moved there at the same time. The records state that Henry became a member of the Christian Church in Corbin. (One can presume his wife Sallie did the same.) Having been a minister himself, he was well accustomed to the need for volunteers in the church. In the Corbin congregation, he served in different capacities during the following years. Other than teach a Sunday School class, whether Henry Masters did much or any preaching after he left the ministry of the Dunkard Church is not known. Members of the family told me they doubted that he ever did. There is a notation in the history of the Corbin church that Henry Masters was elected an officer in 1903. How long he served in this capacity is not known. Other members of the Masters family also worshiped in and were members of the Corbin First Christian Church.

For an aging man, Henry Masters' health was good; his wife's poor health did not match that of her husband. In fact, during the final month of 1907, J.W. stayed close to home because of his mother's illness. By the early part of 1908, she rebounded and he resumed his traveling schedule. Accordingly, he worked in Harlan.

Henry L. Howard, a member of the Harlan congregation, sent a report to the *Christian Standard*, stating Brother Masters conducted a revival in the Court House in Harlan. His comments provide a contradiction: he said there were *no additions*. He did say there were splendid audiences and great good was accomplished. "We had a church building started, foundation laid, framing up, covered, weather-boarded and partly sealed, which was standing there and nothing being done on it for want of funds. Brother Masters aroused the brethren to renewed exertions, and we will be able now, I think, to have our building completed and dedicated sometime in the spring. When completed, we will have the largest and most commodious church building in the [community], and will not have to use the Court House to hold services in." The next statement caused my confusion. "On the last day of the meeting, we organized a Church of Christ with *38 members*." No additions? What about the 38 people who formed a new church?! Sounds to me like a lot of additions. (Incidentally, a statement in Masters' book says the biggest meeting he ever held was in Corbin. In that meeting they had eighty-five additions. That was at a time when the population of Corbin was about four hundred. Compared to the size of the community, the number of new members to the congregation was an astonishing gain! As a matter of fact, 85 additions to any church today would be an astonishing gain.)

Prior to this time, the organizational setup of the Harlan church was weak and inefficient. The church had been in existence since at least 1893. Masters preached for them about once a month during that time. They continued to collect enough money to construct a building. It was a struggle to raise a sufficient amount of money since most of their members were poor and specifically, none of them rich. They had set a goal to dedicate their new church structure sometime in the fall. Sure enough, in September of 1908, the newly constructed house of worship of the Harlan Christian Church was dedicated. Both J.W. Masters and the Secretary of the Board, H.W. Elliott, participated in the dedication.

In the months following, Masters again had to curtail his work in Harlan because of his mother's worsening health. She was expected to die at any time.

Any thought of a tear in the fabric of the Masters family would be a cause of instant sorrow for both generations.

This portrait of the Masters family was obviously taken somewhere prior to 1910, the year of Rebecca Masters' death. Opposite the name of each family member is their birth date.

Masters Family

Front row / left to right:

Sallie Irene	March 17, 1881
Orville Jack	September 2, 1879
John Wesley	January 1, 1854
Rebecca Riggs	February 14, 1856

Back row / left to right:

David Garfield	August 1, 1885
Shelburne Hall	February 17, 1888
Lola Elizabeth	August 15, 1890
Nancy Eunice	December 29, 1891

Coincidental to the time of his grandmother's declining health, Shelburne Masters was giving thought to ministry as a career. Being at his grandmother's house during her illness gave him added time to ponder the thoughts of ministry.

A Third Generation Minister

Shortly thereafter, Shelburne Masters announced to his father that he wanted to be a minister. Both as a youth and as a young adult, I remember a number of occasions when I was in the presence of my Uncle Shelburne. Some of those times were in Corbin at various family gatherings and some of the time he was at our home in Middlesboro when he visited with my father, his first cousin. My great grandfather was described as a tall, rather bald and a somewhat heavy-set man. (I once saw his "Mustache Cup" at my Aunt Eunice's home. The mug was one of those which had been made for a man wearing a mustache.) My Uncle Shelly was likewise tall, but that and his thinning head of hair were the only similarities I remember in the two men. Uncle Shelly was quite thin, never wore facial hair. Unlike his father, as I remember Shelburne's voice was rather high-pitched.

During an interview I had with him in preparation for my seminary thesis writing I asked if his father had influenced him in making his decision to enter the ministry. He said no one had really influenced him. His father said he was the last of his boys he thought would become a minister. He admitted his father found it necessary to correct and chastise him due to unruly or wanton behavior. His burning desire, however, was to be a preacher and nothing else seemed to satisfy him. In retrospect, he surmised that no doubt the fact that his father was a minister did influence him regarding his thoughts of ministry as a career. Shelburne had great respect for his father and regarded him to be a great preacher. Although his grandfather — Henry Masters — had also been a minister, no mention was made of his influence upon my uncle. I knew Uncle Shelly since my boyhood, and before he told me, I had already determined how he felt about his father. He left little doubt that he held his father in high regard. Due to the way he talked about the pattern of his father's ministry, I interpreted such affection and endearment to be the primary pattern and model for him as he envisioned and styled his own ministry. In addition to some pastorates, Uncle Shelly did revival preaching and engaged in

debates in similar fashion to his father.[31] Through the years I have
felt that Uncle Shelly was more like his father than he imagined.
Their similarity was apparent in several ways, not the least of
which was the debating style used by Shelburne Masters.[32]

---

[31] In the summer following my Freshman year at Johnson Bible College,
I drove from Middlesboro to Corbin one night to attend a debate being
conducted by my Uncle Shelburne. The location of the debate was just
across the street from where Colonel Sanders' original Kentucky Fried
Chicken restaurant — now a museum for KFC — is located. There was
a large tent situated on a somewhat triangular lot. People sat on wooden
chairs and fanned with "funeral home fans" to combat the heat. I have
no recollection of the topic or who Uncle Shelly's opponent was in the
debate. This debate was the only religious debate I ever attended.

[32] Recently I received a piece of information about a debate involving my
Uncle Shelly. The story comes from a Johnson Bible College classmate,
Dean Davis, who at the time of the story was minister of the Wilde
Christian Church in Rockcastle County. He and my cousin, Marion
Parkey, were co-moderators of a debate in a church at Cornett's Chapel,
not far from London, Ky., in Jackson County. Dean made references to
my uncle as "Brother S.H. Masters." The debate was between a Church
of Christ minister and my Uncle Shelburne. The topics had to do
with certain beliefs of the Christian Church and the Church of Christ.
Specifically, Davis remembered issues such as the use of instrumental
music in worship and the names of the two bodies of believers. (Neither
of these men would ever have used the term denomination in reference
to their own church.) All the people who supported one minister sat on
one side, and all those supporting the other sat on the other side. At the
beginning S.H. Masters made the statement, "During this debate we're
going to debate issues and not personalities." Not long after he made
his opening statement, the Church of Christ minister began making
comments and even criticisms regarding Brother Masters and something
dealing with receiving money for some purpose. Masters sat quietly and
calmly during this entire time while the other minister went on and on
with critical remarks and the personal attack.

From the beginning of the debate there were a number of charts
relating to various beliefs of the Church of Christ which had been hung
on the walls around the church. The agreement was such tactics would not
be allowed. The ministers had previously agreed to limit their remarks to
specific issues, and not a wide range of topics. When it was Masters' turn
to speak he began by saying, "I want to know who hung all this washing
on the walls tonight?" The audience burst into laughter. His ability to size
up a tense situation and make humorous remarks accordingly, apparently
he learned from his father. The debate at Cornett's Chapel continued for
three nights. Neither side convinced the other of any issue.

The Passing of A Devoted Mother

After a lingering illness, J.W. Masters' mother made her journey to her eternal home. The number of her years, the culmination of her chores, the demands of her large family were all too much for her frail frame to endure. Sallie Riggs Masters died June 23, 1908. Subsequent to the death of his wife and the "breaking up" of his home, Henry Masters moved in to live with the family of his son John. A further move for him within a short time was in changing church membership to the Masterstown Christian Church. Like he had done a number of years before, the change gave him the motivation to serve that church in teaching Sunday School. He continued this endeavor almost until the time of his death in 1921.

A Time to Refocus

Only one who has lost a saintly mother can understand J.W.'s need to focus his attention on things away from home and all that had transpired during the spring. Throughout the remainder of the summer and into the changing fall, J.W. Masters spent his time in Southeastern Kentucky. In an unusual statement in the 1908 Kentucky State Convention yearbook, Elliott reported that Masters had received $494.50 for his services. Mention is made of this because there are few indications elsewhere which refer to whatever compensations this man received for his tireless work on behalf of the State Board of Missions. For what period of time this figure represented isn't known. Was it for the year? Was it for the months only while he was in Harlan or all of Southeastern Kentucky? As I have said before, like all families, money was always a concern for the Masters family. To my knowledge, there were few times when any amount of income was ever mentioned as to what the family received. This is true whether it be monetary contributions or in-kind gifts of food or clothing. If there were such gifts they came from those who were part of J.W. Masters' following. My thinking is a proud man like John Masters would have felt gifts of money, and maybe food would be permissible. I hardly think he was one who would have accepted other sorts of gifts or giveaways — unless it was during the years his children were babes or toddlers. His time at home obviously required his oversight of farm work and whatever produce or like products which came thereby. Not only did he farm as he was able, but part of the children's chores was to maintain the farm.

Throughout this writing I have indicated that it was typical for this mountain evangelist to make reports about his church and preaching activities. Only in retirement did I re-read various reports and materials and discovered something which I had not done earlier. The information had not earlier been important to me. I did not overlook it, it simply had no relevance to me. Then one day, there it was. In the Kentucky Christian Missionary Convention Yearbook of 1908, there appeared the statement that Masters had "worked some in Oldham County."[33] To my recollection, this is the only indication my great grandfather was ever in that section of Kentucky fulfilling the role of minister. I was struck by the realization that for a "mountain" preacher, Oldham County was "beyond the bluegrass." Likewise, for him to travel to Oldham County in order to conduct a revival hardly fit his pattern of revival preaching. Other than his addresses to students and faculty at Milligan College, his sermons and revival preaching had been to rural folks in the mountains. Like the Apostle who committed himself to take the Gospel to the Gentiles, J.W. Masters early on committed himself to preach the Gospel to folks in Southeastern Kentucky. Nonetheless, when he was invited to preach — in the mountains or in the Bluegrass or *anywhere*, it made no difference — he was ready to go preach. Brother Masters made every effort he could to comply with an invitation to preach. I have rethought my initial feeling about his journey to Oldham County. I was wrong, it did fit the pattern. He had no hesitation to preach anywhere, at anytime, to anyone. After all, he had been called to preach.

Beginning in January of 1909, J.W. Masters added Leslie County to his itinerary and began focusing some of his efforts there. He said there were several hundred people who were faithful to the work in that county. The problem was they were without a house of worship. He conducted a revival and subsequently organized the Christian Church at Hyden. At the State Convention in 1909 in Lexington, H.W. Elliott made some observations.

---

[33] Why this incident of J.W. Masters making a trip to Oldham County virtually jumped out at me is the fact that in retirement in 1999, nearly a century later, for a number of months I did an Interim for the Crestwood Christian Church in Oldham County. His time in Crestwood, Kentucky and my time in Crestwood, Kentucky becomes simply one more example, one more occasion, one more way that our ministerial paths crossed or overlapped, so to speak. Sometimes it makes me wonder just how many times this will continue to happen for me in the days ahead. Such a serendipitous experience on the one hand amazes me, and on the other, it sometimes makes me stop in my tracks and ask if there's anything going on here other than a mere coincidence.

Until February J.W. Masters was employed full time and worked in the 11ᵗʰ and 15ᵗʰ districts, living in the 11ᵗʰ. Since then we have had him for half time. He has helped particularly in Harlan County and spent one month in Leslie County. He organized a congregation at the county seat and while we have no house of worship in the County, he reports about 400 members. We ought to have him for full time in that region, and but for the need of seeking to keep our obligations within the limit of our resources we would have continued him for every day in the year.

Between his trips into the mountains of Harlan and Leslie Counties during the year, Masters returned to conduct revivals both at Whetstone Christian Church and Maple Creek Christian Church in Whitley County.[34] The records indicate every year Masters conducted a revival at the Whetstone congregation. I heard one story (essentially the same version each time) from three different sources.

Gus Hill, a Baptist preacher, never attended any of the revival services. Brother Masters was holding a meeting at the Maple Creek Church, and a humorous thing happened. When Brother Masters preached there, Hill would come across the field and sneak up close to the back of the church house, in the cane patch, and would listen to him preach. Brother Masters was told this and he said at the service one night, "I am gonna preach tonight so that everyone can hear — even the fellow out in the cane patch."

Nothing — regardless of how insignificant it might be — seemed to escape the attention of this man. Somehow, some way, he would find and use such information for humor and likewise,

---

[34] I have mentioned while minister in Williamsburg, I conducted several revival meetings at the Whetstone church. What I have not said, however, is that I also conducted one revival at the Maple Creek church.

to include even "outsiders" in the scope of his pastoral awareness and evangelistic preaching.

In the fall that year, Masters went back to Salyersville in Magoffin County, a place where he had lived in his boyhood. While it is possible, it certainly is not probable that J.W. kept any contacts with anyone in that community through the years. Thus, like virtually every other situation, the information about and reputation of this man spread from word of mouth, and church to church. The contact and invitation came from the Magoffin community, and being in agreement, he conducted a revival there.

Masters preaching appointments took him to lots of places in lots of communities. For instance in December of 1909 he held a very successful revival in East Bernstadt, a small community in Laurel County. His usual appointments, took up a goodly portion of his time in Harlan County. Thereby he considered renting an apartment in Harlan in order to better accommodate his lodging needs while in that community. He talked with his daughters — Lola and Eunice — about going with him on his Harlan trips and helping him set up temporary housekeeping. Whether it was a matter of time, inconvenience, other interests and involvement, or something else, Eunice said this plan did not materialize.

David N. Blondell

Through the Valley
of the Shadow of Death

At this time in their marriage, J.W.'s wife, Rebecca, was a woman in her mid fifties. She had always been petite and small of stature. She labored as tirelessly inside their home as her husband did outside. The greatest part of J.W.'s time was spent attending his responsibilities to the State in visiting and ministering to the churches in the southeast sector of Kentucky. By early 1910 Rebecca was beginning to exhibit the signs of what keeping house and raising a large family had done to her over the more than 30 years of marriage. She was not in good health, in point of fact, her health was rapidly failing and it became necessary for the family to devote all possible attention at home. Yet, this was such a crucial period in the evangelist's work in the Harlan territory that J.W. managed to fill two engagements in the month of February. His work necessitated his presence on the field, and he thus sacrificed time away from his ailing wife at home. By giving himself faithfully to his evangelistic efforts, he was rewarded for his successful efforts with the addition of 60 converts to his Lord through his able preaching during this single month.

On March 2, 1910, at the age of 56, Rebecca Robinett Masters went alone through the *"valley of the shadow of death."* Surely through this time she must have *"feared no evil"* because she had experienced many occasions when she faced hardships and dangers alone, holding high the semblance of courage before her houseful of little ones, while their beloved husband and father endeavored, often in far places, to carry out the great commission of his Lord. They called him Brother Masters and he never failed to respond to the call: *"Go ye into all the world and preach the gospel to every creature."* (KJV Mark 16:15)

It is believed that, on the whole, fitting respect has been accorded the men [35] of yesteryear who accepted literally this commandment of the Son of God. Of necessity, these servants were all true prototypes of the term "rugged individualism." To brave the hardships they must face — the loneliness and dangers of the trail, the anger of the elements, the suspicion and hostility with which they were often greeted — they undoubtedly were endowed with the fullest measure of courage and endurance, love for their God and compassion and concern for their fellow human beings. Without their consecration, their devotion to duty and their perseverance, there would have been countless human beings live and die in the remote settlements of the great Appalachian wilderness without ever having heard the message of salvation. The tributes paid them have been justly deserved.

The inconsistencies of humankind — certainly of the American public — are such that while they applaud the actor in the limelight for a well-received performance, whatever the field of achievement, they too often are wholly unmindful of the workers in the background — the technicians behind the scenes whose equal skill, dedication and effort make one's successful appearance possible. The wives of many of the pioneer preachers undoubtedly were such unsung supporters.

The life of Rebecca Robinett Masters was always a tribute to her faithfulness to her husband and his principles. It will be

---

[35] In all fairness to the many men and women who have served the church through the years, it is historically accurate to use only the word "men" in this reflective comment. Thankfully, in the latter part of the 20th century society and the church finally caught up with all the tireless, hard-working, industrious, energetic, and faithful women who for so long had received little or no recognition for their labors along side the men and have begun to give them deserved tributes as well. As a matter of interest, in a "tract" that J.W. Masters wrote, entitled, "Speaking in Tongues," he makes a reference to the amount of good that women were doing. He said they were doing more for the salvation of the lost "today" than were the men. I mention this to indicate one more time that, this is a clear signal of his liberal spirit. Understand, however, that the term *liberal* describes only his attitude and methods in order to proclaim the Gospel — not his theology. Not only did he use whatever he could to further the cause of the Gospel, he also was willing to give credit to whomever it was deserved in the cause of promoting the Kingdom of God.

remembered early in her married life she sacrificed a sizable inheritance because of her faithfulness to her husband's religious convictions. This was done in the face of consequent years of insecurity and financial crises and need for herself and her family. She endured innumerable uprootings, lived among strangers, and made out as best she could through untold difficulties. She bore a large family — seven sons and daughters — and through much of her life was not physically strong. Throughout her adult life, her love for family, her patience in having to do without, and her courage to *keep on keeping on* towered like the mountains among which she was reared in her native Virginia. When I asked my Aunt Eunice, "Would it be true to say that your mother was largely responsible for raising the children, more so than your father?" she replied "Oh yes, it would be true."

It seems fitting that here I avow my profound respect for this unpretentious and all but invisible ancestor whose life story so graphically attests to her trust in the promise, *"Strive first for the kingdom of God and his righteousness, and all these things will be given to you as well."* (Matthew 6:33) Moreover, it is also fitting to acknowledge the children of this amazing pair — all of whom have now gone on to their reward. They too merit an acknowledgment of their sacrifice in relinquishing their normal share of a father's time and attention.

H.W. Elliott reported Rebecca Masters' death to the State Board. "Masters suffered the loss of his wife and hence did little work," in the period following. Acknowledging his singular contributions, the Board agreed to pay him for the remainder of 1910, regardless of the amount of time — or lack thereof — which he would give to the work in Harlan County.

Masters' absence from work because of his bereavement for his beloved wife was forced to be short lived due to the heavy Harlan County program that called for his compassionate attention. Nevertheless, his effectiveness from the pulpit was for a time weakened by his deep grief.

An indication that he wasn't allowed much time for grieving is the fact that starting in July — just over four months after the passing of Mrs. Masters — he held a couple of revivals in one of the numerous small communities in mountainous eastern Harlan County. Mr. H.J. Fee made the official report and told of the results of two revivals at one church.

> John W. Masters of Corbin, closed a week's meeting at Bob's Creek, near Cawood, Harlan County, on Monday, August 27, with 15 baptisms and others having taken membership from denominations. Brother Masters also had a week's meeting at this place in July which resulted in 28 baptisms. When Brother Masters came to this place there was no church here, no Sunday School and possibly 3 or 4 members. Now we have a church with 68 in number, a Sunday School with more than 100 in attendance.

From our perspective in the early part of the 21st century, we stand in awe of the work of Masters and his contemporaries whose accomplishments list such outstanding results in the churches where they preached and where they ministered. We tend to ask, "Was it their personalities?" "Was it their ability to generate true discipleship?" "Was it their aptitude to get members to make strong commitments and develop secure and effective program?" "How could grown men — old men — attract small children and interest them in regular attendance?" "How could their numbers be so small and their results so large?" We are all aware the times were different, simpler, slower, less complicated. The level of response though, was just as necessary because resources were fewer, the need for volunteer time was equally as real then as now, available income was on a much smaller scale for giving to the church and other benevolent causes instead of always paying bills. Faith and faithful commitment to the church always brings on questions, lots of questions and sometimes not many answers.

David N. Blondell

Return of the Yearn to Evangelize

In the fall of that year, he preached the One Hundredth Anniversary of the Whetstone Church with the largest crowd anyone could remember.

In the fall of 1910, J.W. Masters attended the State Convention in Owensboro. During the gathering H.W. Elliott introduced the evangelists who were present. Along with the others, Masters was introduced and made a brief speech. Whether or not he had done this at other state gatherings, or whether he was chosen to represent the others, we are left to supposition in the matter. It is significant to note, however, unlike most other times this mountain evangelist was the only evangelist to speak. Out of great respect, it could be he was selected for this assignment by his fellow evangelists. It could be they chose him because of the tremendous work he had done even though through it all he had labored with a heavy heart. It is not known whether or not he was the senior member of this fraternity of evangelists, and thus spoke accordingly. His remarks were devoted principally to the work he was doing in the Southeastern part of the state. While he and the others who worked on behalf of the State Board were called evangelists, much of what they did was primarily pastoral in nature. Principally, that means they devoted their time to only one congregation.

By this time J.W. Masters was beginning to feel a strong pull away from the constancy of the pastoral responsibilities of the work in Harlan County. He let it be known he wanted to spend his time wholly to evangelistic work. As the word got around, the Harlan County people did not want to relinquish their devotion for this man. Such an outpouring of affection for him indicated his influence was needed in the work in Harlan more than he realized. The insistence of the people convinced him that he should not leave them completely, so he continued to spend time there until the close of the year.

In the early part of 1911, the members of the Harlan congregation and the man they knew and called Brother Masters worked out a compromise regarding his time in their community. It was decided Masters would preach half time for the folks in Harlan and also devote half time to evangelistic work elsewhere. Masters relied heavily on his son, Shelburne Masters, to carry on the work in Harlan County. This is the first mention of any kind of ministerial responsibility Shelburne fulfilled.[36] During the summer and fall of that year, J.W. intensified his responsibilities by dividing his preaching time between the churches in Harlan and Laurel Counties. Through the efforts of this pioneer preacher, he continued to add many people throughout a good portion of Eastern Kentucky to the Restoration Movement.

At the fall 1911 convention of the churches of this rapidly growing movement, Masters was again in attendance. When presented to the convention goers in Frankfort, along with the other evangelists, again this year he made a short presentation outlining his work and his love for the people in the Southeastern region of Kentucky.

Because of hazardous weather conditions and equally hazardous roads, Masters had great difficulty at the beginning of 1912 in traveling in Harlan County — even on horseback. As the wagon and buggy traffic became heavier, making passage through the Harlan County trails was no easy task. Members of the family often remarked about the number of horses he had in his years of travel.[37] But despite the difficulties of travel, he reported amazing results. Secretary Elliott recorded that he organized a congregation at Crank's Creek and started it with 62 members — 19 of whom were baptized and 10 came from other "fellowships." Mr. Elliott stated that this made 7 congregations in Harlan County, whereas only a few years previously there had been none of the Christian Church persuasion. It is not clear

---

36 Among the mountain communities, three things seemed to qualify one for ministry. One was the validity of a call; a second was the strong desire to do ministry. A third was experience. Of course, adding to these the addition of some theological and/or academic background would further qualify one as valid preparation for ministry.

37 Perhaps this statement was another way of saying what Masters himself said when he made reference about how hard it was to make ends meet. He wrote that on four occasions he preached himself afoot.

from this statement alone whether J.W. Masters was responsible for the establishment of all these churches or merely helped in their organization or re-organization. The implication is he did organize these churches. A listing of the known churches which J.W. Masters organized is in Appendix C.

In early 1912, the State Board discussed the possibility of securing Masters' services to work in Russell, Adair, Casey and Wayne Counties. When all parties were in agreement, it was arranged for him to start in June. The agreement was that J.W. would go to Russell County where there were 5 congregations. None of the five, however, had regular preaching or Bible schools. While he was still quite successful in his preaching in both Knox and Laurel Counties, including a tent revival in the west section of Corbin, during the next several months Masters worked heavily in Russell and Clinton Counties, with surprisingly few results.

A person's sense of enthusiasm and excitement seems to reach a little higher when presented with a new challenge. Moving from deep in the hills and mountains of Eastern Kentucky, the response to his efforts in his new field of endeavor seemed not to match from those among whom he labored. How long he retained his level of excitement isn't known, but surely the low numerical response did not help either.

The Old Life with A New Mate

It was in the latter part of 1912 that Lila Stinson became of singular importance to this mountain preacher. On her return to her home in Williamsburg, following an out-of-state visit that summer, young Miss Stinson accompanied her father to a revival at the Whetstone Church to hear John Masters preach. She later learned that Masters had written to her first cousin, John Stinson (father of Dave), inquiring about her and her whereabouts. In 1962 I had the privilege to meet Mrs. Masters and visit with her. She spoke freely about Mr. Masters and any occasion when she heard him preach.

> I didn't know that he knew anything about me. We always went up there to hear him preach — all of us. I never thought about ever going with him or ever thought about him, any more than just a preacher. I went back home, and he wrote me a letter. My oldest brother told me that while I was at Sunday School he had gone to the post office and brought me home a letter. As I read it I thought it was the funniest writing I ever saw.[38] The letter read, "I know you'll be surprised to get a letter from me. But while you are the one who might be surprised, I might be the one who will be disappointed." I didn't answer it for quite awhile; I tried to keep it a secret as to who had written me.

Mrs. Masters told me of the sequence of events that followed. After a time she answered the letter.

---

[38] In my visit with Alonzo Masters, J.W.'s nephew, he told me his Uncle John was the minister who performed the wedding ceremony for him and his wife. He said his uncle told him his writing was so poor he wanted Alonzo to make out his own marriage certificate. Alonzo said he knew of his uncle's handwriting and knew why his uncle asked him to do so. He gladly complied.

The next thing I heard from him, he wanted to come down to Williamsburg. He wrote again saying that he would come from Corbin soon. He left on the 7:00 o'clock train and came to the Williamsburg hotel. Jim Vaughn was then managing the hotel. Mr. Masters was acquainted with him... [each reference she made of him was always "Mr. Masters."] He sent a note up by John French's boy that morning. I was getting some apples off a tree there in the yard. The note stated that he would like to come up right away. I sent an answer to him by the boy, telling him to come by at noon for dinner.

John Masters visited Lila Stinson that day and on other occasions during the next few weeks. My Uncle Shelly told me in the fall of that year his father went on a two-months' journey to Oklahoma. This was in response to a request from his very close friend, D.T. Chestnut. Uncle Shelly remembered some of the particulars of the trip.

Chestnut had moved to Oklahoma and was running in a political race. I do not remember just what office he was seeking, but he wanted my father to come out there and hold some revival meetings. In the meantime, he asked him to speak a good word for him in his race. While there, my father conducted two revivals. He held one in Lawton and the other was in Oklahoma City.[39]

---

[39] Perhaps this sort of thing happens to all ministers, but again I found this information of my great grandfather going to Oklahoma quite intriguing. Sometime in the early 1980s, I attended a meeting of the National Evangelistic Association (NEA) of the Christian Church (Disciples of Christ) in Oklahoma City, OK. I was assigned a particular family with whom I was to stay for the 2 or 3 nights I was there. What I did not know was this family had requested the leaders of the NEA to allow me to stay with them. They informed me their congregation was interested in having me become their minister there in Oklahoma City. We talked about the possibility one evening but I declined their invitation. I have always regarded this connection with Oklahoma as just another coincidence. You guess?

While in Oklahoma, J.W. wrote to Lila. She recalled that the letter said, "You be ready when I return, because I have to go to the mountains and I will take you with me. I do not want to go by myself." That is how J.W. Masters' proposed to Lila Stinson.

When I was pastor in Williamsburg during the late 1950s, Mrs. W.R. Mounce, Sr., one of the elderly members of the church, told me that the wedding took place in her home. At the time I had not yet decided on the subject for my seminary thesis and made no notes of the conversation with Mrs. Mounce. Thus, between her comments and those of Mrs. (Lila) Masters, I have only included details of those things which I remember. Accordingly, this is how that transpired.

Mrs. Mounce said Lila Stinson crossed the street to her house and asked if she might get married there. Because of the considerable difference in the ages of her daughter and Brother Masters, Lila's mother was not in favor of the intended marriage. Although wishing no trouble with her neighbors the Stinsons, Mrs. Mounce consented and gave permission for the wedding to take place at her residence. John Masters and Lila Stinson were married in Williamsburg, Kentucky on November 15, 1912.

Responses to the Restoration Plea

On November 26, shortly after their marriage, J.W. Masters and his bride left their home in Corbin to go to Clay County for a revival. Mrs. Masters recalled their first night on this trip was spent with a preacher named Scott. After the evening with the Scotts they went to Coon's Creek for a two-week revival and stayed with J. Hugh Morgan. As she put it, during the revival he "captured" a Baptist preacher and twenty-six of the members in that meeting in a school house. Masters related the same story in his book.

> I held a meeting in a section where the Baptists had a congregation, and we had only a few people. The pastor of the Baptist Church lived among his people and heard every sermon. On Sunday morning my subject was "Christian Union." Just before I called for the invitation song, I said: "You Baptist people are cordially invited to unite with us on the Bible alone. If you will not accept the invitation, let your preacher make the same proposition to us and we will accept it. This proposition means, when we start to you we leave behind us everything that is not in the Bible, and when we get to you everything that you can't show in the Bible, throw it out of the window." Then the song was begun. The preacher led the way and his flock followed him. We organized a church of Christ that night and the preacher was made pastor of the new congregation.

Interestingly enough, there was another very similar circumstance involving a Baptist congregation and the subject of Christian unity. It included the principle of uniting on the "Bible Alone." This time, however, the preacher was opposed to the proposition. In *Following the Trail...*" Masters recorded the occasion.

I was called to dedicate a house of worship in a small town, and hold a meeting. One night I preached on the importance of the Lord's people being one. I tried to show that this old world will never be brought to God by a divided church. The following Saturday was the Baptists' regular meeting. I attended. I got there before the preacher came.

A young man of the Baptist Church sat down by my side, saying: "Brother Masters, I am impressed with the proposition you made the other night. I believe we Baptists ought to accept it." I had made this proposition: "We as a church are willing to unite with the Baptist Church on the Bible alone." I said: "I wish you would." The young man then said: "I will make a motion to that effect after our preacher gets through." I said: "A better way is to write it and read it to the church." "That is what I will do," said he. He wrote as follows: "We, the Baptist Church of this town, accept a proposition to unite with the Christian Church, that we may be able to employ a more competent pastor."[40]

After the sermon he arose and read as above stated. The preacher said: "Let me see that." He took it, looked at it, and threw it on the floor, saying: "Away with it." There was one more time there for about an hour. Finally the young man's father said: "This is a new thought to me. Let us postpone it for a month, and study the matter. I believe it is the thing to do; we ought to unite." The preacher was as mad as a "wet hen." He said: "Preaching to-morrow." I said: "Brother, if you will have no services in the morning, we will have none at night,

---

[40] And they were surprised when the minister did not accept the term, "more competent pastor"?

and we will worship together." "I will leave at two o'clock to-morrow." He never left until Thursday morning. He remained to guard his flock.

Wednesday I was stopping at a merchant's home, and an old Baptist brother came and told me there was something up at the blacksmith's for me. I told him to bring it to me. He brought nine sheets of a common-sized writing-tablet written and pinned together. I asked him who wrote it. He answered: "The blacksmith said the preacher wrote it and left it for you." "A Catechism for Campbellites" was at the top of the first page. Then the question, "Who baptized Christ — John the Baptist or Alexander Campbell?" The balance was questions and no answers.

That night the church-house was filled and the preacher in the center. I tried to get him up to the front, but he stuck to his seat. One of our elders came up on the rostrum and said in a low tone: "We have decided that you had better say nothing about that written matter to-night." I said: "You go back to your seat." He said: "What are you going to say?" I answered with a smile: "It is none of your business." At the proper time I arose, took the manuscript from my pocket, and held it in my hand for a few minutes, saying nothing.

Finally I said: "I don't know just what this is; it claims to be a catechism, but it is not. A catechism is a book of questions and answers. The questions are here, but no answers. I don't know who wrote the little thing. Yes, I guess I do. At least, I am reminded of a circumstance that happened during the Civil War. A soldier during a bloody battle left his rank and the colonel said, 'Come back to your post.' The soldier said, 'I am afraid.' 'I would not be a coward,' said the colonel. 'I am a coward, and they ought to have let me alone at home. The colonel said, 'I would not cry like a baby.' The soldier replied, 'I wish I was a baby, and a gal baby at that.' I guess that a gal baby wrote it. The next morning the preacher passed some little boys on the street. The boys said: 'Yonder goes the gal-baby preacher.' So that gal-baby preacher took the first train going his way. I continued the meeting a week longer, baptized twenty-four and captured twenty-four Baptists. I went away rejoicing over truth's victory.

In 1913, Masters held revivals in several communities in Whitley, Laurel, Leslie and Perry Counties. Thereafter he traveled to Wayne County and Pulaski County to conduct revivals. Lila Masters told me about the meeting Masters conducted near Somerset, at Science Hill.

He had me come to him at Irish Bottom. I went by train this time, he wrote me to meet him at Mill Springs. I got off the train at Burnside. After that, we went to Monticello in Wayne County and talked with Brother Rethmeyer. Brother Rethmeyer sent us out in the country about twenty miles. This time we made the trip in a buggy, and a young black man drove us over there. We didn't do any good there because there were too many anti-organists.[41] We stayed only a few days, and went back to Monticello. We then went to Norwood (near Science Hill) and held a meeting.

The recollections of Mrs. Masters in our visit were confirmed by H.W. Elliott.

---

[41]   Mrs. Masters used the phrase, "anti-organists" in referring to what today is known as the Churches of Christ, non-instrumental denomination. The historic conflict among the three branches of the Stone-Campbell Movement — Churches of Christ, Christian Church, and Christian Church (Disciples of Christ) — has been well documented elsewhere.

Humor, Revivals and Strong Preaching

Tom Lay, Shelburne Masters' brother-in-law, told me of an incident he had with the elder Masters. The circumstance was one Sunday morning when J.W. conducted the morning church service without the dignity afforded by his usual custom of wearing a suit coat.

> J.W. Masters was at my father's and so was I. My wife was in the hospital in Lexington. On Saturday night a drummer[42] came along and I took a notion I'd come on to Junction City with him in his buggy and then on to Lexington from there. I was at the store and my coat was hanging out in the hall and so was Uncle John's. I just jumped out of the buggy and ran in and grabbed a coat and we came on to Junction City. I stayed all night at a hotel and got up Sunday morning and found out that my coat was big enough for an overcoat. I do not know what Uncle John did for preaching that day because he surely could not wear my coat.

In the summer Masters conducted a revival at Jamestown, Ky. where his son, S.H. was the minister. (Publicly and professionally, my uncle was referred to both as S.H. and Shelburne. The family mostly called him Shelly.) Uncle Shelly remembered this incident.

> After services that day we went home with a family for Sunday dinner and after dinner the man of the house said, "Brother Masters, the Holiness people are having a revival out here under a brush-arbor, would you like to go out about 2 o'clock this afternoon?" He said he would. We went out there

---

42   The term "drummer" is not used today in the sense it was years ago. What we call a commercial traveler or traveling salesman today is what they called a drummer.

and when we walked up there were about seven people down in a circle, praying. And one of them got up and picked up a Bible and walked across and handed the Bible to an individual at the far end and said, "Here, the Holy Spirit has selected you to preach today." Well, the Holiness preacher preached about an hour and fifteen minutes. After they dismissed we were walking down the road. There wasn't a word said. Then I asked, "Father, how did you like that sermon?" He said, "Son, I think the Holy Spirit made a bad selection."

Later in the summer of 1913, Masters held revivals in Casey County and Adair County. At the time Uncle Shelly was newly married, and accompanied his father, as did both their wives, to the revival in Knifley, in Adair County. Both of these ladies and the minister of the church were all red-headed. Someone commented there was "quite a combination of redheads" in attendance that night. From such a comment, it is easy to see there was a sense of openness and freedom in those days during church services which is not always present today. While humor was not unique with them, this does give another glimpse of how humor was sometimes part of worship.

Speaking of worship, J.W. Masters delivered the opening sermon of the convention of the churches in the London District, held in October, 1913. Generally, he attended these meetings, but this time he was the keynote preacher.

In his annual report that year, H.W. Elliott indicated Masters again traveled to Oklahoma and spent two months in the fall preaching in revivals. As always Elliott was very complementary in his remarks about Masters' "strong preaching."

Regardless with what difficulty this giant in the pulpit started out many years earlier, there is no doubt J.W. Masters became a tremendous preacher. Nearly everywhere he preached, scores of people came to hear him — usually they wanted to be near the front of the church, courthouse, or wherever the assembly took place. I am confident the attraction of this man and his preaching was not because folks were curious as to what they would encounter in the man. Their quest was obviously to hear his sermons and the straightforward manner in which he delivered the plain gospel which underscored everything he did. It was like wanting front row seats at mid-court in a championship game between the top teams in the conference. Wherever he held revivals (or meetings as they were mostly called), he was sought out for advice and counsel. Although he was getting rather old to continue at the pace he set for himself, nevertheless, at this time his health was still fine. At sixty years of age, he continued to preach and carry the same load he had during the previous ten to fifteen years. Remember what he did in January of 1907? Remember that he "preached 55 sermons" in one month?!

By 1914, word about this man had spread well outside the bounds of Southeastern Kentucky. One such example was when he preached in the northeastern part of the state, in Greenup County. Gone were the jokes about his stuttering and stammering and inability to preach. Gone were the antics he had relied upon in those beginning years to get through the delivery of a sermon. Gone were the days when the visitors were the ones who came to see if he would falter or stumble in his preaching due to a speech impediment. Gone were the days anyone wanted to see how well he spoke, or whether or not he was still plagued by the speech demons that accompanied him early on. As a matter of fact, I do not remember ever hearing any member of the family say anything about his mature years of preaching. My hunch is he was never bothered by the earlier condition and stigma.

By this stage in his life and career, the reputation of John W. Masters focused on a man who rode tall in the saddle and stood tall in the pulpit. His strong, fundamental preaching was not mere rhetoric. The character of his Lord and the contents of the scriptures were the focus of his sermons.

He had come a long way from the novelty he once had been. John W. Masters was one of the most able defenders of the Restoration Plea in Kentucky in the early years of the 20th century.

Traveling South and Back

Several months prior to his father's trip into Greenup County, Shelburne Masters moved to Decatur, Alabama. A move to a new location always means settling into the location, becoming acclimated with the community and members of the church. Not being a product of that generation, I am in no position to assess the style of pastoral leadership of ministers in those days. My instinct, however, tells me the role of preaching received the greatest amount of ministerial attention in lots of smaller congregations. Thus, having assessed the needs of the membership and confident of his father's preaching skills, Shelburne contacted him and asked him to come to Alabama for a revival in the spring of 1914.

J.W. told his son he would like to do that. First, before accepting the invitation for a revival he needed to clear arrangements with the State Board through the Secretary. Taking time away from his leadership and preaching responsibilities with the churches under his charge is one of the indications of the flexibility he had with the Board. His understanding with the Board allowed him to step back from his regular duties and appointments to do some "free lance" preaching in another venue. The matter was so recorded in Elliott's March report. Masters was granted time to be out of the state in the spring in order to conduct a revival in Decatur, AL.

Uncle Shelly said the revival meeting with his father was very good. "We had 52 additions and he baptized 51 of them." As usual, the revival's success was impressive not simply to the folks in the Decatur community but also in surrounding areas. That became evident in succeeding years when J.W. Masters was recalled four times to that church and others in the area to conduct revivals.[43]

Upon their return home from Alabama, J.W. and Lila Masters began house-keeping in West Corbin. In a revival a short while after this, Masters became acquainted with Cleo Purvis. Mrs. Masters talked about this occasion.

> At that time the church in Corbin was without a minister. Mr. Masters saw that Brother Purvis was a very shrewd young man and that he knew his business pretty well. He spoke to the brethren about Brother Purvis. Purvis came for a visit and we were to meet him when he arrived on the train. I said, "You just go on and I will not go. I will stay here and prepare supper." But he said, "No, you are going with me." I said, "Well, there is no sense in it." But we walked down to the depot. Mr. Masters said, "the ugliest man you see coming around that train will be Brother Purvis. He is a man that favors Abraham Lincoln." Well I picked him out and he told on me after we got back home. [One of the most successful pastorates in the history of the Corbin church was during that of Cleo Purvis.]

It was during this year, that H.W. Elliott also was a visitor in the Masters' home. According to Mrs. Masters, Mr. Elliott came for a visit with the congregation on Sunday. He arrived for his visit on Saturday afternoon and spent the night. He was

---

[43] What shall I say? I do not intend to sound "like a noisy gong or a clanging symbol" and go on and on with the subject of *"I went where he went"* kind of thing. But I simply need once again to comment about another path my great grandfather and I crossed during the course of our ministries. From 1964 to 1968 I was the minister of First Christian Church in Florence, Alabama. During some of that time a Johnson Bible College classmate of mine — Jerry A. Smith — was minister at the Decatur church. It was my pleasure on a number of occasions to be in Decatur for District church meetings of one sort or another. During March of 1967, I was asked to conduct a revival at First Christian Church, Decatur, AL. Again, if this kind of thing is only a coincidence, then so be it!

the guest preacher for the church Sunday morning and returned home later that day on the evening train.

As was almost always the case, whenever an evangelist went into a community he would stay with the host pastor. Such was the case with Mr. Masters and the Whetstone Church. Whenever he was in that community, as I have mentioned before, Masters always stayed in the home of John Stinson. The following comment by Dave Stinson who lived at home during those early years shows how this seemingly tireless preacher used any available opportunity to conserve energies for his strenuous work.

> Late in the afternoon he would generally get out on the porch. We had one of the old cane-bottomed rocking chairs and he would sit down in that and would read until he would almost doze off to sleep. Then he would say, "Brother John, I am going to have to get up and move around." Mother knew just how to fix his supper as much as she did for the rest of us. He would not eat too much before he went to preach; but whenever he came back from church, that is when he wanted something to eat.

Mr. Stinson shared with me information regarding something of the amount of income Grandpa Masters received for his ministerial services either from the State Board or from additional preaching services with the many congregations where he preached. We have noted many times, the amount he received for his services was never quite sufficient to meet his needs. Like anyone else, any supplementary income always was a help for him through difficult times. The following account of another incident when Masters endeavored to pursue some sideline service in order to acquire additional income comes from Dave Stinson. I never heard of this particular event from any other source — family or otherwise.

He took on a sideline of selling glasses. He would carry his little glass case and whenever he ran across somebody who needed glasses, he would make them a fit. He did not just fit different glasses until they found one that suited. Rather, he had the instruments to give eye tests. Thus, he made proper fittings. He would go up to the Post Office and sit around. When different fellows came in needing glasses, he would fit them. He would fit up several pairs at a time.

H.W. Elliott's report at the 1914 Convention included comments regarding the expanding preaching services Masters was called upon to perform. For instance, during this time he preached at the church in Maysville, in Mason County. The Board of Missions organized the whole state into a number of districts. Elliott made reference to the work of these District evangelists. Specifically, he commented on the work of Masters. "While J.W. Masters lives in the 11th District, his work is not confined to that section. He does work in many parts of the state and does it satisfactorily. He is a strong evangelist."

Masters tried to make as many of the state meetings as his time and schedule would allow, but he was not always present. Whether or not he was present at the convention in 1914 is not clear. On Tuesday morning of the convention, however, Elliott introduced the workers of the field, and made this statement. "J.W. Masters who preaches in Southeastern Kentucky, began work in the mountains 29 years ago and is now living in Corbin." That tells of the long and lasting association this mountain preacher had with the Christian Church in Kentucky.

A Command of the Scriptures

That J.W. Masters and H.W. Elliott had a long and successful association is well documented. Among other things, it was based surely upon performance in the field as well as relationships with communities and one's stature among peers. Likewise, there was also the same kind of association between Masters and the Christian Church in Kentucky. From the very beginning, one of the trademarks of this Pioneer to the Mountains was his thorough acquaintance with and command of the scriptures. That's why the next story from *Following the Trail...* catches my attention and reflects his sense of timing and quick wit.

I began a meeting at the mouth of another creek. One morning, just as I was ready to read my text, some one handed me a note from a Baptist preacher, asking me to repeat a certain sermon that he had heard me preach... and give him thirty or forty minutes to reply, I accepted his proposition. When we met [I presume upon another occasion] there were seven other Baptist preachers present. When the time came to begin I preached as though I was not expecting anyone to answer me. I closed, telling the preacher that he could have the floor. He got up and placed another preacher at a window with a Bible. The speaker had a paper in his hand with his Scriptural references. When he called out book, chapter and verse the man at the window turned to it and read.

Finally he called for the thirty-seventh verse of a chapter that had only twenty-eight or twenty-nine verses in it. The reader turned and looked, turned and looked; his face got red. I said: "Brother, just read the thirty-second verse; it will do," He angrily said: "There is no thirty-second verse here, and you know it." I said: "Yes, and you ought to know it." We had a good time for about three hours and closed. One of the older preachers said: "I told them to let this alone. I am glad that they got a licking. I guess they will listen to my advice the next time."

At the beginning of 1915, Masters continued the concentration of his labors in Harlan County. He had only five additions during the month of January. The work during February and March was no more profitable as far as numbers were concerned. The work of ministry in general and that of an evangelist in particular is not always able to be measured by immediate results. Such was the case with the arduous work of Masters in the Harlan area over long periods of time. During this stretch of time whatever effort he put forth went without visible results. In April his work began to experience a remarkable turnaround; he had twenty additions. By the first of June, the church in that community was able to employ a full time preacher for the Harlan territory.

During one of his meetings in the Harlan area, Masters preached a sermon on the topic, "*Talking With Tongues.*" The sermon was most likely preached during this period of his time in Harlan and had a tract printed with the same title. A copy of it is reproduced in Appendix A.

My Uncle Shelly told me that in the early summer of that year, his father held a revival in Wayne County near Monticello.

> The name of the place was called Seventy-Six; in fact the name of the church was Seventy-Six. It was right there close to a seventy-six-foot waterfall in the creek. Then after that, he held a meeting at Creelsboro. Seventy-Six was in Wayne County and Creelsboro was in Russell County.

In July Masters traveled to Jackson County to conduct a revival. His report to the State Board indicated there were seventeen additions, thirteen of whom were by baptism.

When he returned home from a meeting or a series of meetings, Masters would share the events with his wife. Mrs.

Masters told me "Mr. Masters" would not only tell her about what went on during the time he was away, he also expressed to her his attitudes toward various other matters, such as politics. Her comment indicates she was quite opinionated herself and not afraid to voice her thoughts to her equally strong husband.

> He was a strong Republican. One of our neighbors was running for a public office. Although George Lawson was a Democrat, nevertheless, Mr. Masters wanted to vote for him because he was a member of the Christian Church. He said to me, "Let us go vote for George Lawson." I said, "What is George?" He said, "He is a Democrat." I said, "Well, I am just going to cross my vote." He said, "But he is a brother in the church." I said, "Well, if he is a brother in the church, he ought to be a Republican."

In telling me this, she laughed heartily. It was obvious both of their statements indicated no ill feelings toward members of another political party. If there had been any strong bias, they would not have made comments in a light-hearted manner as they did.

In September 1915, J.W. Masters again journeyed South. This was the second year in a row in which he was asked to come to the churches in Alabama for revivals. His son, S.H. continued his ministry in Alabama, and no doubt served as a contact person and helped set up the meetings in the communities where his father preached.

According to information that came from the Regional office of Kentucky, in those years the State Board of Missions engaged the services of forty-seven men to preach and do support work for congregations throughout Kentucky. Of course none of these roaming, traveling evangelists was full time with the state work. The thought, however, that the region of Kentucky even on a part-time basis employed the services of forty-seven preacher-evangelists is a staggering thought. In the work of the Regions of the Christian Church (Disciples of Christ) today, there isn't a single Region that comes anywhere near engaging that many people part-time or full time to work with the local churches. In a statement at the 1915 State Convention regarding the tremendous task certain of the workers were performing, H.W. Elliott singled out four men from the forty-seven. These men were J.S. Dean, D.Q. Combs, W.J. Hudspeth, and J.W. Masters. Commenting about their collective work, he said, "these men have spent much of their time preaching regularly for churches." Then, regarding the work of Masters individually, he said:

> J.W., Masters has been at work for many years in Southeastern Kentucky. He gave himself for a few months to the work in Harlan County after the leaving of C.A. VanVinkle. The remainder of the time he has been in the evangelistic field of that section and really was at work in Harlan [town] in the same way. He has given the gospel to many sections of the hill country and many there are who rise up and call him blessed.

It was no news to anyone that the people in that section of Southeastern Kentucky dearly loved "Brother Masters" and he dearly loved them.

During the early part of 1916, Masters spent a large amount of his work in the adjoining counties west of Corbin, which was still his home. His preaching for a struggling congregation in this field was soon to result in a new building. According to Elliott, Masters additionally preached and worked in Pulaski and Lincoln Counties. J.W. was confident that he would be able to raise enough money to build a church. As was the case a time or two before, no one knows which church Elliott intended by his remarks.

S.H. Masters returned from Alabama to Kentucky during the latter part of 1915 to accept the pastorate of the Mt. Moriah Christian Church in Lincoln County. He had been the pastor of the congregation in Decatur for the better part of two years. After his move back to territory that bordered the Bluegrass, he engaged his father to hold two revival meetings for him later that spring at the Mt. Moriah Church. The first meeting resulted in little gain, but the second was a huge success. All in all there were sixty-four responses to the preaching of J.W. Masters — four by baptism, four from other sources and the remainder came by letter: "reclaimed" or by statement of transfer of church membership. He organized a church in Lincoln County and raised funds for building a "house." Since the Mt. Moriah congregation was already in existence, his work resulted in the formation of a new congregation.

In the early summer of 1916, Masters was asked to come to the First Christian Church in Corbin and hold a revival. It was a happy occasion for him to revisit and preach for this congregation which had long been dear to his heart. The meeting resulted in twenty-three additions.

In the fall, for the third year in succession, Masters was out of state for a one-month period involved in revivals in Alabama. He conducted the revivals either with churches where he had previously preached, or at least in that general area.

Like the Ripples in A Pond

The 1916 Convention yearbook of the Christian Church (Disciples of Christ) in Kentucky, states — with the exception of the Midway congregation which gave support elsewhere — the churches in Woodford County gave financial contributions that year to support the mountain ministry of J.W. Masters. Then as now, churches gave financial support to various kinds of mission work. Disciples churches these day identify this giving as either local or world outreach. It is likely a number of state evangelists received funds from various churches. It is a point of interest that financial support from these churches in areas which are a considerable distance from the mountains, indicates the work of these evangelists, and principally that of J.W. Masters (for our purpose in this writing) was sufficiently appreciated and thereby recognized as worthy of financial support. Word regarding the valid and solid ministry in the mountains spread like ripples in a pond.

At the close of 1916 Masters returned to hold an evangelistic meeting in Lincoln County at Crab Orchard. While there, he wrote to his nephew Alonzo R. Masters, making a brief comment about the meeting. The main purpose of his letter was to relay some information to his brothers, William and Dave. He had located some land in Lincoln County and wanted them to know about it, in the event they might be interested in making a purchase. Several times toward the close of 1916, he also preached at Preachersville in Lincoln County. He held a revival meeting in Rockcastle County in December. This revival was held either at the Christian Church in Wildie or in Mount Vernon. (I mentioned my roommate one year at Johnson Bible College was Dean Davis. Dean was minister at Wildie at the time.) Years later, my cousin Marion Parkey served as minister of the Mount Vernon congregation. When I was minister in Williamsburg I remember going with some of our members to a service at the Mount Vernon church when Dr. Fred B. Craddock was preaching. As we visited, I talked with some of the members that night who remembered my great grandfather. Some had heard him preach many years earlier.

In March of 1917, Masters wrote an article for the *Christian Standard*. He reported about the completion of a revival at Cornett Chapel, in Jackson County. In April he went to Clay County to conduct a revival in Manchester. They had a building but the congregation showed signs of weakness and were without organizational structure. He agreed to conduct a revival for them. His brother, William, attended a service one night during this revival. William told his niece Eunice what happened.

> William said one night when Papa was preaching there were several boys present. They kept getting up and going out of the church. Then they would come back in. Once, when two or three of them came back inside and sat down, my daddy said, "Boys, you know, when I was your age, the reason I got up and went outside during a revival was because I did not have any socks on and I had to get up and go out to warm my feet around the fire." Bill said there wasn't another one to go outside that night. [My father once told me that Grandpa made a similar comment to some young boys doing the same thing at another revival. "Boys, I understand what you're doing and it's okay with me. If I had the "itch" and had to go outside to scratch, I'd do exactly what you're doing." The results were the same — there was no more going out and coming back in that night.]

For the remainder of the spring and summer of 1917, Masters preached for rural churches in Wayne, Jackson and Clay Counties. Part of that time, due to personal sickness he was not able to do any church work or revival preaching and was confined to his home. In July he improved sufficiently and was able to hold another revival at the Manchester church. He later preached for a few weeks in Monticello and also continued his general evangelistic efforts in Southeastern Kentucky. Elliott reported to the Board "the most conspicuous single work done by him was in the resurrection and reorganization of the Manchester Church." There is no question — as in a number of other places — the Manchester congregation regaining its strength was due to the tireless efforts of J.W. Masters.

By the fall of 1917, Shelburne Masters had become the minister of the Christian Church in Kings Mountain, in Lincoln County.[44] As he did in each of the other churches where he served, in October he arranged for his father to hold a revival in Kings Mountain. Uncle Shelburne said they had a good revival with "excellent interest." In spite of inclement weather both in November and December, J.W. worked diligently in Clay County, resulting in fifty-three additions. Like he had done in so many other communities, he organized a congregation at Fogertown. He also helped make arrangements for a preacher to begin serving that church on a regular basis. Things went so well they immediately made plans to build a new building.

---

[44] Upon graduation in 1957, another college classmate of mine, Erwin Ray, became minister of the Kings Mountain congregation. He told me he and S.H. Masters lived in sight of each other's house. "I have a vivid remembrance of a funeral service which Bro. S.H. Masters and I had for one of our neighbors who also lived at Kings Mountain. As a young preacher just out of Bible College, I was impressed with the way in which Bro. Masters handled his part of the service. He used no Bible. He quoted each reference he made to the Bible. He was well versed in the Bible. I remember sitting in his front yard under a shade tree and listening to a man who knew the Bible from cover to cover. He was one of those remarkable persons who was well advanced in age and yet had a great memory. He offered his library to me, but not having much money in those days I felt I would be taking advantage of him if I accepted his offer, and I refused to take his books. He knew he was getting older and what he really wanted was to give his books to some young preacher. Looking back on the situation, I now know if I had taken the books I would have honored his wishes." (Parenthetically, I have often wondered if Grandpa Masters gave his son Shelburne any of the books from his own library. As my friend Erwin said, "Just think of some of the great books he must have had!" In reference to that, in his tribute, J.C. Eagle said Masters "accumulated a large library of good books authorized by the ablest preachers, who stood firmly for the restoration movement of New Testament Christianity.")

As far as was practicable, the Masters families kept in close touch with each other. Age and years did not alter this practice for the Masters brothers. I made reference earlier that J.W. had sent word to his brothers advising them about the availability of some good land near Brodhead, in Lincoln County, Kentucky. In former years J.W. had always preceded his brothers in these incidences of relocation. This time it was Dave, Wilson and William who made the move and settled in Lincoln County sometime in 1917. Thus, early in 1918, J.W. likewise followed their move to Lincoln County. He and his wife relocated in Crab Orchard.

During 1918 J.W. devoted the greater portion of his evangelism efforts to the work in Clay County, particularly in the Manchester community. His longtime friend and colleague, H.W. Elliott visited the Manchester church in July and commented about his visit.

> We have a house there which was built in 1887. For years it was not used by our people at all — or, at least, very irregularly. More than a year ago J.W. Masters went there and succeeded in starting work afresh. They have about 20 members. The town is growing and new people are moving in. The location of this community is at the terminus of a new bit of railroad, twenty-five miles long, going out from Barbourville. Brother Masters wrought a fine work in starting afresh the Manchester congregation. He is making plans for a meeting by one of our strong men, and is hoping to be able to locate a man to preach regularly there and in other parts of the county.

In addition to his work with the Manchester congregation in Clay County, Masters did part-time preaching at the Livingston Christian Church in adjoining Rockcastle County. In late summer he broadened the scope of his work in order to devote more time in both Rockcastle County and Whitley County.

Time to Pull Back on the Reins

Year in and year out J.W. Masters enjoyed excellent health, even though now he was approaching age sixty-five. Nonetheless, he was aware that one day soon he would need to pull back on the reins and begin to conserve energies for health sake. As fall approached, he realized he had taken on more than he should have and his load was heavier than he was able to manage. He did some preaching in various churches in August, but during September he became too ill to preach. A simple glance at the accounts of his work — his travels, his revival schedule, his debating and sometimes with more than one opponent at a time, not to mention the enjoyment he derived in doing farm work at home when he was able — was all enough to dictate it was time for him to begin slowing down. His age and the pace he had set for himself was beginning to show whether or not he wanted to acknowledge it. For a time he remained at his new location in Crab Orchard, Kentucky. When he had an opportunity to spend time at home, regardless of how brief or how long that was, he did some gardening. He had taken breaks in his work in previous years, but now it became necessary for him to spend more time at home in an effort to regain his strength and stamina.

The State Convention in 1918 was held at Richmond, Ky., not a long distance from Masters' residence in Crab Orchard. The awareness of the short distance, however, was not enough to entice him away from the needed time at home for rest and recuperation. His strong desires to the contrary, because of illness he was not able to travel the short distance to Richmond and attend the convention with his fellow evangelists. It is noteworthy to mention, even with a somewhat reduced schedule of travel during this year, J.W. Masters received from the State Board the amount of $825 for his services. This was the highest amount of financial compensation he ever received for a single year for his work associated with the State Board of Missions.

In his annual summary of the work of the evangelists at the statewide meeting of the Christian Churches, H.W. Elliott gave an account of their efforts. His comments to the assemblage relative to his friend and colleague, J.W. Masters, simply said he had continued in the Southeastern part of the state in the role of General Evangelist.

The sickness that Masters had during September was somewhat preliminary to the epidemic of influenza that swept the country a short time later. Because of the widespread effect of the pestilence, he traveled into the mountains only a part of the month of December. At the beginning of 1919 the epidemic raged almost without control across the nation and overseas. Whole families were wiped out. Hundreds of thousands who recovered suffered lengthy illnesses. The public health agencies enforced strict quarantines. During this year there was a marked decline in church statistics throughout the state. Masters, when not ill himself, like all other ministers during this period, was performing a ministry that was truly applied Christianity — serving however and whenever he could to offer comfort and compassion to his fellow constitutes far and near during this time of national peril. The 1919 Kentucky yearbook contained the following statement.

> Perhaps at no time for thirty years have our results been as small as for the year closing September 1, 1919. This is due in a large measure to the interference of the influenza epidemics when the churches were closed for a long period and no public assembles allowed. There was hardly a protracted meeting held in Kentucky for six months. Very many communities had no schools for much of the time and even where the churches had been opened the attendance was small. We call attention to the fact that the salaries of all our men were paid in full, even when they were unable to preach. Many of them were at work among the sick and distressed, as were the preachers generally. Some of our men are regarded justly as heroes.

This was the general picture across the Commonwealth of Kentucky during the major portion of the year 1919. Among the few meetings held during the six-month period mentioned by Elliott, some of them were conducted by J.W. Masters. Earlier that year in February, he conducted a revival and welcomed into the church twelve additions. At the same time there were communities in his territory that had no meetings due to insufficient numbers of people who were able to attend. Every community had different stories to tell. In a singular experience in one Harlan County community, when he went into one mining town he found it deserted because of the closed mines. When the mines were down, everything was down.

March of that year again brought sickness to Masters. He was able to get out and go some during the month, but for the greater part he was confined to his home. In order to lighten the load and lessen his traveling time by horseback, or merely to stay in close touch with his brothers, in early May he moved from Crab Orchard to Gum Sulphur, in Rockcastle County. His brothers, Wilson and Dave, as they did the previous time, again had already made the initial move ahead of him. Mrs. Lila Masters told me when they were still in Crab Orchard, Mr. Masters learned of some land in Rockcastle County. When her husband became well enough he bought a strip of land from his brother Wilson. In the spring they moved to Gum Sulphur.

Many of his friends in Corbin had been asking him to return and preach for the churches there. He continued his schedule in the areas in Lincoln and Rockcastle Counties, but agreed to return to the Corbin area and also preach in some of the former communities where he had done so previously. A local historian in Corbin reported that, "John Masters, now of Gum Sulphur, but who, until recently, resided at Corbin, is expecting to preach in Southeastern Kentucky this summer. Brother Masters, in spite of his advanced age, still preaches most of the time."

By the summer of 1919 Masters was well enough to be out and about and again active in conducting revivals. In June, one of his meetings was at the Goshen Christian Church in Lincoln County.

In response to my question about her late husband's feelings concerning World War I, Mrs. Masters told this incident.

> He really did not express his feelings too much. The only time was when he sent a German to meet me at the train depot and take me to Mr. Masters. He told me, "I am sending a man to meet you, do not be afraid of him. He is a German. But do not say anything about the War." He was holding a meeting out from Stanford, where I caught the train. I do not remember the name of the church, but he has held several meetings there. [She made no other comment pertaining to his or her thoughts about the War.]

In July he held a meeting in Madison County at Speedwell. It is not likely that he ever conducted a revival in any other church in this county. In his travels he passed through Madison County, but no other revivals are mentioned. Thus, the following story told to me by my Uncle Shelly about a revival in Rockcastle County seems to fit either preceding or just following the revival at Speedwell.

> There is a minister who lives in East Bernstadt who used to live outside of Richmond. One time when my father was there in East Bernstadt for a revival meeting, the old man told me after the meeting concluded he brought my father back to Richmond to catch a train to go home. My father was always fond of fiddle music. A fellow was sitting there in a chair at the station. He was leaning against a post, playing the fiddle. My father stood there looking at him and became so engrossed in the man playing the fiddle that the train came and left, and he never noticed it. He had to go back with the man and stay at his house until the following day. He made sure that he caught the train the next time.

Later that summer in August, J.W. Masters made his fourth trip into the state of Alabama to conduct two revivals. In a conversation with Uncle Shelly's brother-in-law, Tom Lay told me the revivals were at "Albany and LaCon." There was a community known as Albany, but it no longer exists. The same is true with a small community named LaCon.[45] Both the *Christian Standard* and the Kentucky Convention yearbook attest to this trip to Alabama. Here are Mr. Lay's remarks.

> In 1919, I was in Alabama when Mr. Masters held a revival down there. There were several churches close together, enough so that I could hear each of the others from where I was sitting in one church. When Brother Masters got up to preach he said, "If we could all get together, I could preach to everybody in Albany and Decatur just as easily as I can preach to this little handful. But I do not think that the people will ever unite unless we preachers all die. After about thirty years the people would then all get together. But as long as we preachers have anything to do with it, this will not happen because we have to have jobs. Therefore, we have to keep the churches split."
>
> Then he held a meeting at LaCon, not far from Albany, in Morgan County. One street divided the two communities. This was on the same trip because I was never down there more than one time. Chief Jones and I were there. Brother Masters

---

45   Mr. Lay was mistaken about the towns in his story. He told me Decatur was changed to Albany, actually it is the other way around. Albany became part of Decatur. Most likely it was a small township on the border of Decatur, and in time became incorporated into the Decatur city limits. Likewise, when he mentioned LaCon, he was evidently speaking of another small community just south of Decatur, on US Highway 31 near the Morgan and Cullman County line. LaCon no longer exists. This small village is like other small communities in many parts of the country. Time and Interstate highways (I-65 in this case) have virtually bypassed these villages and they have become the proverbial wide-spot-in-the-road.

told the two of us that if we would come to church
with him he would pay us for coming.

The comment by my great grandfather regarding the reasons
for division in the church caught my attention. I'm not sure just
what he meant by "all the churches getting together." In some
respect, however, it reflected a genuine concern and perhaps
some insight into his view of the problems of Christian Unity. It
is obvious he laid the greatest blame on the clergy of the day for
divisions within the body of Christ. In regard to this matter of
unity and disunity, he was speaking interdenominationally. He
frequently commented about divisions and disunity within the
body of Christ.[46]

When he returned home from the trip to Alabama, he gave
himself little time for any "R and R." Determining himself to be
in sufficient health, Masters spent a beneficial month in Harlan
County. There were twenty-eight additions to the church during
his preaching at the time. Part of these additions — if not all
— were the result of a revival he conducted at Grays Knob. In
October he conducted two revivals in Casey County: one at
Dunnville, and the other at Piedmont.

As 1919 drew to a close, the folks in Jackson County
invited their favorite mountain preacher to be their guest for a
revival. He accepted the invitation. The meeting Masters held
there in December was tremendously effective. The interest
and enthusiasm for that time of the year was unusual, and the
number of additions — forty-eight — was remarkable. As usual,
his preaching and the results there-from caught the attention and
gained the appreciation of Secretary Elliott.

---

[46] I have earlier made reference to a brochure/tract that my Grandpa
produced, *Speaking in Tongues*. Again I would call attention to Appendix
A where he makes the following comment. "The question is not what we
must do to become a Campbellite; a Methodist; a Baptist; a Presbyterian,
but what must we do to become simply a Christian. God wants us to be
Christians and nothing more." As far as I can determine J.W. Masters
never believed any point of view than the one which held out for the
unity of all of God's people. He contended for this position throughout
his life.

Still... "A Power for God"

In the spring of 1920, J.W. Masters continued to evangelize Southeastern Kentucky. He also preached occasionally at his resident church in Gum Sulphur, in Rockcastle County. A report in the *Christian Standard* demonstrated how this man could put courage and a renewed spirit into a congregation that had all but closed its doors. The report stated that Masters organized a congregation at Gum Sulphur, Rockcastle County with 43 members. They began meeting regularly in an abandoned house. During the same time he raised enough money to put the house where they were worshiping in good order. They made plans for a rededication later in the season. The report emphasized Gum Sulphur was the only church in this railroad village.

In typical fashion, during the year Masters still devoted some of his efforts to out-of-state revival work. In one of his personal date books (which was given to me and is still in my possession) Grandpa noted he held a meeting in May, 1920, at Boone Creek, Tennessee. A Mr. G.W. Settle, a member of the Boone Creek congregation, in Jonesboro, TN, remarked about the two weeks revival at the Boone Creek Christian Church, conducted by "Brother J.W. Masters." There were "twenty-seven additions to the Lord — twenty-four by baptism and two from Baptists, one from the Methodists. Brother Masters is a power for God." A characteristic which we wished belonged only back in time — "additions to the Lord: from Baptists and Methodists" — is still prevalent today. Too many times anyone transferring from one congregation or denomination to another is received with equal zest just as if they had no previous church affiliation. *Is it possible that the preachers are still to blame?*

When he returned to Kentucky from any out of state preaching, Masters always accounted for what he did, where he went, how he spent his time, and the results of his work. Since he didn't usually make such a comment relative to finances, of particular interest this time is his reference to the money he received while he was in Tennessee.

I closed the fourth meeting with Boone Creek Church, Tennessee. This church is about six miles north of Johnson City. For the period of a 17 days' meeting, with 24 baptisms, 2 of which were from the Baptists, 1 made a confession and is not yet baptized, they paid me $202, or $52 more than I ever received for one meeting. These good people love the Plea of the Restoration. They are for no other movement."

Such a commendatory statement for just $200 seems an almost paltry amount of income in this day and time. Nonetheless, it was a substantial amount to one doing *"the work of an evangelist"* in the mountains in the early decades of the last century.

For twenty-four days during the month of June, Masters was engaged in a meeting at the Mount Olive Christian Church in Jackson County. In early August, he made what would turn out to be his last trip into Alabama. This was his fifth time to be called to one or more of the churches in that state for revival meetings. This time his destination was Falkville, Alabama. He preached for four weeks straight, from August 12 to September 8. By this time John W. Masters was 66 years of age. I mean not to over emphasize the point of this kind of preaching schedule, but the grinding pace he set for himself, regardless of the high he obviously received from the opportunity to preach the gospel he loved to preach, must have been difficult to say the least. After all, preaching five or six nights a week — plus, as we have seen in several of his accounts there were also morning preaching events during those revival days — for a period of four weeks straight is a most demanding requirement for one even at a much younger age! Is it not true that regardless of the number of additions during a revival, the mere fact that this aging servant of God was able to fulfill such a commitment was a huge success in itself!

H.W. Elliott recorded in the state yearbook that Masters had devoted about half of his time through the year to the churches in Southeastern Kentucky. As a consequence, his work always brought good results. He noted that Masters was employed on a regular basis by the State for two Sundays each month. He commented on the meetings he held in Tennessee and Alabama. He said he was there for two months, "and was far better paid than he is in Kentucky. He has some good results to his credit."

J.W. didn't necessarily admit to tiring from his many travels and much preaching, yet toward the end of 1920, he began to draw to a close his specific work as an evangelist in Southeastern Kentucky. It was at that point he decided not to accept invitations to do evangelistic work during the next year. Rather, he determined he would work regularly for a few congregations. As his employer and close friend, Elliott said he was "entitled to some let up in his strenuous work for few men have worked harder in the field than Masters." In the same report, Elliott said Masters had dedicated the new five-room church at Wallins Creek, Harlan County, and raised the money to pay for it.

The winter months were getting harder and harder for the aging Masters, given the fact that unlike others who went to work down the street, across town, or even at home — the work of an evangelist was to go the distance: miles or counties or a state away. Besides that, again this particular winter, ill health was a factor for him. During part of February 1921 he was unable to do much work. Although his pace was not as it had been in previous years, nonetheless, John W. Masters answered the call to preach even at times when common sense said he should not. Yet, it was on such an occasion when he recorded this comment:

> I was holding a meeting in a neighborhood in which was a sick man, and at his request I preached one night in his home. On account of a continued rainfall, many of the neighbors spent the night there, and among them was a Methodist preacher. I proposed to retire, but the preacher wanted an argument before retiring. I was tired and needed rest, and did not think that an argument would amount to much, but the Preacher was full bent on having his way about it. He would ask questions; I would dodge and propose to go to bed.

Finally he opened his artillery and leveled down on me with the question: "Do you believe in the mourner's bench?" I said: "No; are you ready to go to bed?" He said: "I believe in it, and will tell you why I do. I went five nights to a revival meeting which did little good, so I quit going. My friends got me to go back, and the very first night I was converted. It seemed everything beneath me was going away and that I was falling down into the dark pits. It seemed everybody in the house was happy, and the trees around the house were praising God, and I was then converted." I said: "Are you ready to go to bed?"

He, however, wanted to convince me and asked: "I would like to know what you think about it." "All right," I replied. "What made you feel like everything was giving away and you were falling, and everybody in the house happy and the trees praising God?" He answered: "The Spirit." I said: "I know; but what spirit was it? You will surely not claim it was the Lord's Spirit that thus falsely impressed you. It was a false spirit. The Spirit of God makes only true impression on the human heart." He answered: "I am ready to retire."

Through the remainder of that year, although authorized by the State Board to do evangelistic work in many sections of the Commonwealth, Masters continued to carry on a devoted ministry to the folks of Harlan County, particularly in Wallins Creek. From 1903 until this time J.W. Masters had preached literally thousands of sermons and received literally hundreds of members into the church in this section, and the people here were very dear to his heart. For J.W. Masters the dear folks in Harlan County constituted the "tie that binds our hearts in Christian love."

David N. Blondell

Closer and Closer to Home

For more than 10 years the elderly Henry Masters — ever since the death of his wife Sallie — had been living in the home of his son J.W. At nearly 90 years of age, Henry Masters passed away in 1921. Though he had long since completed his work of ministry, the elder Masters' mission ended in the village of Gum Sulphur, KY. For whatever reason, his father's passing seemed not to interrupt for very long John Master's customarily busy schedule.

J.W. Masters is a prime example of one who does not take well rest and relaxation. Today we refer to such a practice as recycling or retooling. It was true at each point in his life when he lost a loved one — his mother, his wife, his father. Either he did not take much time to find rest or he was one of those individuals who needed little time to rest. At the same time it just may be that keeping busy was his way of coping with the loss of someone close and dear. It is obvious he had an inner strength, an inner source of energy, some connection that moved and motivated him that does not seem available to everyone. Or it simply could be that he was attuned to a higher power, whereas most of the rest of us are either not listening or simply identify with that power when it calls. Whatever time he took, whatever time he needed, John Wesley was ready, willing and able for the next challenge.

J.W. said he wanted to keep closer to home during the next year and was not going to do revivals during 1921. Nevertheless, when the Casey County Mount Olive Christian Church invited him for a second revival in as many years, he responded affirmatively. He preached the revival in the month of August. It was a surprise to no one that the new minister of the Mount Olive congregation had considerable influence on this evangelist. It was further no surprise that Brother Masters accepted the offer to preach the revival. The foregoing statements are made on the basis that by that time Shelburne H. Masters was the new minister of the Mt. Olive Church. It is possible Shelburne was also pastor at the church during the 1920 revival meeting. Like his father, S.H. Masters reported his work. Without remarks pertaining to the evangelist being his own father, S.H. made reference to the 1921 meeting.

> There was a good meeting held at Mt. Olive church, Casey County, during the last two weeks of August. The revival was conducted by J.W. Masters. The meeting resulted in 38 additions — 25 baptisms, 2 came from the Baptists, 4 took membership and 7 renewed their fellowship with the church.[47]

In the late months of 1921 J.W. Masters found time enough to put the finishing touches to his beloved work at the Wallins Creek Church. At the close of the year, H.W. Elliott's annual report to the churches included remarks relative to the decision to conclude his work in that congregation.

> J.W. Masters closes his work at Wallin's Creek, Harlan County, where we have helped in his support. He expects to give a good deal of time to evangelistic work, and could be had by some churches in reach of him.

Through the year of 1922, J.W. served the South Corbin Christian Church as its pastor. How much time or how many days per week were required on his part is not known since he still maintained his residence at Gum Sulphur. It obviously meant he did some commuting from one place to the other. By April the work at South Corbin had grown and attendance at the services

---

[47] This report was made to the Board of Missions and raises the question whether or not he too was engaged to work for the Kentucky State Board of Missions of the Christian Church. It could be he simply found the reporting procedure to be a good way to promote the work done at the Mt. Olive Church. It is entirely possible he made the report the way he did because the visiting minister was his father. He knew of his father's popularity and knew others were always interested in knowing what Brother Masters was doing and where he was preaching, and would joy in the good results of his work.

had doubled. The interest was manifested in their efforts to build a church (or as he would prefer to say — "a house of worship"). There was hope that an early dedication would be possible. By midsummer, however, normal activities in this railroad-center town were largely at a standstill because of a prolonged crippling strike among the railroad shopmen. The church was "compelled to defer dedication on account of the strike." Plans were formed to hold the dedication in October but whether or not that took place on schedule could not be determined. Maters issued an invitation to Elliott to be present and deliver the dedicatory address. Sickness in Elliott's family, however, forced him to decline the invitation. Masters continued to serve as pastor of the South Corbin Church until the first part of 1923.

At the age of 68, Masters spent a strenuous month during August of 1922 preaching his fifth series of evangelistic services at the Boone Creek, Tennessee. Insofar as determined, this trip to Tennessee was the last labor for his Lord he was able to perform outside Kentucky. He commented about this revival.

> The third Sunday night of August I closed my fifth meeting for the church at Boone Creek, Washington County, Tennessee, with 20 baptisms. Boone Creek brethren are true to the Book, and will have nothing less and nothing more. I love to preach for such people. I hope to be with them again. I love them.

"My Years of Activity Will Soon End..."

In retrospect, J.W. Masters gave indications to his family that in 1922 and 1923, he demonstrated an urgency for completing various projects which had received major portions of his attention in previous years. His determination to work as diligently as he could, both in Harlan County and in Corbin, was evidence of such intentions. Most significant, it seems, was the writing he did during the busy year of 1922 and the publication of the short volume I have mentioned so frequently. He fully realized his ministry had been a full one. He was aware of the many experiences of consequence he had performed in numerous mountain communities in Southeastern Kentucky. Likewise, he had performed tirelessly in other places where he carried the message and banner of the Restoration Plea. He felt content with the mission that had been his to perform.

From the beginning to the end, he had been a man dedicated to his calling. The events most vivid in his memory and those which stood out as most important, he recorded in his book, *Following the Trail of a Preacher in the Mountains of Virginia and Kentucky for Forty-Seven Years*. I do not know what prompted him to write the book. Maybe it was at the insistence of members of the churches where he preached and those to whom he had been pastor. Maybe it was encouragement from members of his family or from his friends. We all have had moments when either we or someone else has said, "I should have written a book." Maybe he was responding to a personal compulsion to leave for posterity a glimpse into the immense panorama of his activities for his Master to whom he had labored since the days of his youth.

The book was published in 1922, but we neither know where, nor by whom. Characteristic of many undated, undocumented pieces of history during those years, it might be questioned as to how the exact date of this writing was determined. The solution is found in the last paragraph of the book. There is the simple statement: *"Kind, reader, I now take my leave of you. I have lived my threescore and eight years, and I am aware of the fact that my years of activity will soon end."* Knowing therefore that he died in 1924 at the age of 70, the small book was published two years earlier.

On March 26, 1923, J.W. Masters and his wife Lila moved once again. This time it was to the small hamlet of Lily, in Laurel County. The Lily community is approximately midway between Corbin and London. Mrs. Masters told me she had been dissatisfied throughout the time they lived at Gum Sulphur. She said, "Mr. Masters was not satisfied either." The fact was she had been by herself too much of the time. "I didn't like to stay there by myself, and went with him when I could. But when we moved to Lily, we were both very well satisfied."

Mrs. Masters told me about the end of 1923, she accompanied her husband to a Homecoming event in Nicholasville, Ky. There is no account indicating for which church this event was held. Going to Nicholasville was their last trip together.

When it came to fulfilling his call to preach, John W. Masters knew no limits, had never accepted difficult circumstances as reasons to fail to preach, did not have "no" in his vocabulary. As far as humanly possible, Masters journeyed wherever he was called to preach the gospel of Jesus Christ. For several years, he had preached frequently for his son, Shelburne. In 1924, either in August or September, he preached a two-week revival meeting. Uncle Shelly told me, "The last revival he held for me was when I was preaching at Brush Creek, just outside of Liberty, in Casey County. At that meeting, he had forty-five additions. At the close of the meeting he stood in front of the people and said, 'I am not tired yet.' When he left to go home was the last time I ever saw him."

It was a kind fate that led J.W. Masters, late in September, to preach in the mountain village of Trosper, Knox County, Kentucky, near Barbourville. This was the immediate section to which he had come to preach when he traveled from Virginia to Kentucky some thirty-eight years earlier. From beginning to end he answered the call to preach. In this revival he gave his last full measure of devotion in a one week evangelistic meeting. This was to consummate his lifelong mission for his Master.

Grandpa Masters had no idea anything was wrong with his health. Afterward, he went home and died.

Mrs. Masters told me any time he had been away preaching, when he came home he would continue to do his farming.[48] She told me the circumstances of the events which occurred that hot Ocotber afternoon the day he died.

> In the fall of that year he hired a man to sow rye for him but the man had run out. At that time Liza [J.W.'s only sister] was staying with us. Well, Mr. Masters went up to sow seed in a short strip of land. We asked him not to go. It was a hot October day. Liza and I were at the house and it was after noon. We were getting a little uncomfortable about him. Liza went up to the top of the hill to take him some water. That is where she found him. He was lying in the field. He died of high blood pressure.

---

[48] On one occasion J.W. wrote to his nephew stating he had a good piece of land near Brodhead, Ky. that would make 15 to 20 bushels of wheat per acre. This kind of reference is interesting since farm land in this area was some of the best soil in Kentucky. Evidence supports the reality that most farmers working larger portions of land in Kentucky, then as now, devoted their land, time and efforts to raising and producing tobacco. Obviously, such was not the case with this conscientious steward and sometimes-farmer.

The End of an Era

On October 3, 1924, approximately at midday, John Wesley Masters finally found rest for his restless, passionate, servant, obedient soul. The following article appeared in the October 9, 1924, issue of the London *Sentinel Echo*.

> Rev. J.W. Masters, dean of the Christian Church ministers in South Eastern Kentucky and beloved by all within and without the church, died suddenly last Friday while in a field at his home at Lily, near London. Rev. Masters had preached in many communities in the State and was at one time the pastor of the London church. He actively engaged in the work of the church until his death.

> The deceased was a native of Virginia. Funeral services were held in Corbin Sunday in the presence of many hundred sorrowing friends.

Gilbert E. Chandler was the minister of the London Christian Church at the time and delivered the funeral oration. This beautiful benediction to the life of this devoted servant, *A Tribute to A Pioneer*, appears in Appendix D.

With a most fitting quotation from the book by John W. West, *Sketches of Our Mountain Pioneers*, I conclude this account of the life and work of J.W. Masters: able preacher, worthy debater, tireless evangelist, devoted servant, and beloved family patriarch.

> Wit, humor, and logical thinking made him a power to be reckoned with. With the truth on his side a denominational preacher was left floundering in embarrassment when debating with him, or in any combat.

It is well to recognize that he was not seeking debates, but ever ready to accept a challenge and to defend what he believed with his whole heart to be the truth. He preached the gospel in all its fullness, without fear or favor. He was not afraid he would offend someone by preaching the truth, but fearful he would displease his Lord if he failed to declare the whole counsel of God.

These pioneer preachers, like Brother Masters, never faltered in convictions, but stood like a stone wall for the truth as it is revealed to them in the New Testament. Their children in the gospel were many.

CONCLUSION

At intervals during the writing of this account of the life of my great grandfather I have made quotations of the number of additions to the church as the result his work. I have commented on the amount of money paid him by the Kentucky State Board of Missions for his services in communities where he lived and worked. I have done this in order to show how the amount fluctuated. In a reference I made pertaining to the 1918 State Convention in Richmond, Ky., it was mentioned the highest amount of money he ever made in a single year was $825. At the other end of the spectrum, G.E. Chandler, who gave the funeral oration for Masters, comments that "for a ten days' meeting he was paid a quarter." The full text of Mr. Chandler's remarks are in Appendix D.

I have not given the total number of additions or amount of money which was mentioned in reports by my great grandfather and his friend and colleague H.W. Elliott. There were month-by-month reports and quotes from the *Christian Standard*. Since all the reports were not available, the information would have been incomplete. Therefore, I have included a summary of highlights of the work he did for the State Board reported between 1908 and 1921, in Appendix B.[49]

As an introduction to Masters' book, H.W. Elliott wrote an overall summary of his work with the churches of Southeastern Kentucky during the years of his ministry with the State Board.

> During twenty-two years,[50] beginning with 1893, with gaps of several years at different times up to the present, he added 3,270 in all ways to the church, helped at more than two hundred places, organized nineteen churches and received from the Board $9,900. This represents what was paid to him by the Board and does not take into consideration the amount he received from the field for his services for much of the time. He has lived a life of sacrifice and has wrought much for

---

[49] The categories found on that summary page are quite indicative of the thought pattern of that day. It will be noted there are several *membership* categories such as "letter or statement," "reclaimed," and "other sources." Those simply indicate, I presume, ways that members were added to the church other than by confession of faith and baptism. In quotations from his book sometimes he used the term "capture" to refer to additions. He mentioned "churches aided" and "preachers located" which seemingly had to do with his personal assistance in providing help for churches and securing permanent pastoral leadership for a particular congregation. The one which I find of singular interest is the one "churches set in order." One can only surmise what the term means specifically, but it seems probable that some kind of incident had taken place and an outside source was called in for a possible disciplinary action. Whatever the case, I found several of these categories of significance.

[50] Using the records of the State Board of Missions, I compiled a list and produced a table in Appendix B, showing a compilation of various categories J.W. Masters reported to Secretary Elliott. This list includes a period of 16 years, from 1908 to 1923. A couple of those statistics virtually jumped out at me! For the 16 year period he preached 3,342 sermons! (This includes 1919 — the year of the flu epidemic. During that year he only preached 150 sermons!) Another statistic stands out; over that same 16 year period, he collected from the congregations the sum total of $3,258 for himself. That figure includes merely $150 during 1919. Obviously Mr. Elliott had fuller records to draw from, but I was astonished by the low figures of income relative to the days worked on the one hand during that period, and on the other, the huge amount of sermons preached.

the cause of our Lord. He is large in body, mind and heart.

> Thousands of the people in the hill country of Kentucky, Tennessee and Virginia will read with much pleasure these pages [Masters' book]. While it is the story of a very small part of his labors, the writer wishes that its circulation may be large.

The foregoing summary, however, included only the work done by Masters in his ministry in Kentucky. This statement by Elliott included nothing after the year of 1922. The detailed record covers only twenty-two years. It is certain the ministry of J.W. Masters — stretching out for nearly fifty years — yielded much more than is shown in those statistics.

I remember the occasion in 1957 when family and friends gathered at the cemetery in Corbin for the dedication of Grandpa's monument/headstone. Along with others, my cousin Marion Parkey, my Uncle Shelburne Masters and I participated in the Sunday afternoon graveside ceremony. (A full account is in Appendix I.) I drove to Corbin from my home in Middlesboro early that afternoon. Both of my great aunts (Eunice and Lola) and my uncle Shelburne were still living and present. As Marion reminded me in a note he wrote to me several years ago, his mother, my Aunt Lola, sat with others in the family under the tent at the grave site. Aunt Eunice was not well enough to get out of the car and walk to where a chair had been arranged for her. Consequently she remained in the car with the door open so she could see and hear the graveside ceremony.

As I said at the beginning, I considered the life and work of my great-grandfather John Wesley Masters, to be an appropriate subject for my seminary thesis. I grew up with an image of this rather mythical ancestor who was a stuttering, joke-cracking, debating primitive preacher. By the time I had finished the thesis, I had gained an appreciation for an entirely different, more mature, more productive, more saintly servant of God.

A great amount of the work and influence of this dedicated servant has been obscured by the passing of time. The quantity of evidence I found over forty years ago was virtually unbelievable, and convincingly tips the scales in his favor. I merely scratched the surface in making whatever effort necessary to accumulate such information. The lasting worth I derived from that endeavor — and it has become even more meaningful to me in this current endeavor — lies in the fact that I came to know, not the legend of the J.W. Masters I had heard about from various members of my father's family, but I touched the heart and soul of the man himself. I am proud to claim him as ancestor and humbly acknowledge he was indeed a saintly man.

In his tribute and eulogy to Masters, G.E. Chandler noted something which might easily get pushed aside in all the accolades made. Commenting about his nature and strength of character and faithfulness, Chandler said, "Nature in her angriest moods sent floods and storms, and still he went; he never missed an appointment; he never turned back." When I attempt to imagine how he struggled to "keep on keeping on" I am amazed at what this man accomplished for the sake of his Lord.

In my initial writing, my feelings for the man I had heard of since childhood increased a hundred fold. In revisiting that first experience, I can now say that my respect, my admiration, my esteem and my gratitude for everything about John Wesley Masters is more than I am able to convey in words.

APPENDIX A

A Tract Sermon, "Talking with Tongues"
Rev. J.W. Masters

No subject demands honesty and sincerity on the part of the people more than the one that has to do with our future destiny. I enter upon the task before me conscious of the fact that I will have to account of the Judgment for what I write on this subject as well as for what I say in the pulpit. Friendly reader, you will have to account to God for the disposition you make of what appears on these pages. I therefore beg you to give these thoughts an impartial trial by the Bible. From my boyhood, I have heard preachers tell their hearers, that they need to be baptized with the Holy Spirit, and that "The baptism of the Holy Spirit is the main baptism." It seems to me that "Holy Rollerism" is the result of this thought. Good people plead for the baptism of the Holy Spirit, and yet they deny the results of it. What were the disciples baptized with the Holy Spirit for on the day of Pentecost? They were already pardoned, pure and cleansed, and even had the power to heal the sick, cast out devils and raise the dead. Matthew 10:8.

Then what were they baptized with the Holy Spirit for? Jesus had commanded them to go and preach the gospel to every creature. Mark 16:15. How could they do this, seeing they knew not the language of every creature? Jesus said "Tarry ye in the city until you be endued with power from on high" Luke, 24:49. Power to do what; they have the power to go, and to preach, but they could not preach the gospel to every creature, they lacked this power. This was the power they were commanded to wait for. In Acts 1:4-5, the Baptism of the Holy Spirit is spoken of as the promise of the Father. See also Matt. 3:11. The baptism of the Holy Spirit was the promise. And the ability to speak with other tongues (Acts 2:4.) was the power for which they were to wait. The prophecy of Joel (Joel 2:28) was fulfilled on the day of Pentecost. See Acts. 2:14-18. We in this age receive the Holy Ghost by obeying the Lord. Acts 5:32. We need the Spirit of Christ, Ephesians 5:18. "Be filled with the Spirit." Romans 8:9. "If any man have not the Spirit of Christ he is none of his." The Apostles being baptized with the Spirit preached the gospel in about seventeen languages Acts. 2:5-11. The language in which the Apostles preached was plain and was understood by the people and the result was great. Acts. 2:42-41 When God wanted Moses to lead his people out of bondage Exodus 4:2-7 why did he not have him (Moses) to take the Bible along and show them that such had been predicted instead of giving him power to do miracles? There was no Bible at that time.

Why did Jesus give his disciples power to heal the sick, cast out devils, and raise the dead, Matthew 10:8. instead of having them to take the Bible along as testimony? There was no Bible yet. In Mark 16:17-18, Jesus said, "And these signs shall follow them that believe; in my name shall they cast out devils; they shall speak with new tongues; they shall take up serpents; and if they drink any deadly poison it shall not hurt them; they shall lay hands on the sick and they shall recover." To whom does the foregoing passage apply? The Apostles did such miracles. They spake with new tongues. Acts 3:7. They healed the sick, Acts. 5:15-16. The viper fastened on Paul's hand but no hurt. Acts 28:3-6. Do you know of such being done today? We have the lame as well as the sick around us, and with us. Poor fellows would be glad to get rid of the burden of getting about on the crutch, and go leaping and praising God. Acts 3:8. The Apostles healed the sick and the lame. Acts. 8:7. Now brother show up or hush up.

Why did God give the church the power to speak with tongues, to heal the sick; to interpret tongues, to prophesy and do miracles. 1 Corinthians 12:8-10? Why did he not let them just prove their preaching by the Bible? There was no Bible. Their preaching was confirmed by these miraculous endowments. Paul said, "Tongues are for a sign not to them that believe but to them that believe not." 1 Corinthians 14:22. These Christians not only spoke with tongues but prophesied and did miracles. Do you know of any one who can do such things now? If so bring him around and I will find the man who will be glad to lay aside his crutch. As to tongues, a brother was commanded to speak two or at the most three and that by course; and let one interpret; if an interpreter was not present, keep silence was the order. 1Corinthians 14:27-28.

You will notice that the women were not permitted to speak, only the men, 1Corinthians 11:5. The Christian women of today as a rule are doing more for the salvation of a lost race than men are doing. Back to the subject.

How long were the miraculous demonstrations to continue? Until they came in the unity of the faith, Ephesians 4:11-14 What then? They were to cease, 1 Corinthians 13:8. The Bible being then completed, the preacher was to study and thus become able to divide the word of truth, 2 Timothy 2:15. We are not permitted to preach anything now except that which was preached by the Apostles, Galatians 1:8-9. The world needs nothing more than the plan found in the New Testament. By reference to 2 Peter 1-3, we learn that he has already given us all things that pertain to life and goodness. In 2 Timothy 3:16-17, we learn that the inspired Word of God or Scriptures are profitable for doctrine, reproof, correction, old instruction in righteousness, and that we are furnished to all good works. What more do we need?

If a man should tell us something now in tongues or otherwise that we do not have in the Bible, likewise it would be useless. If it is in the Bible, likewise it would be useless. It would not be safe for an Angel from heaven to preach what we do not have in the Bible. See Colossians 1:8-9. Then away with the new revelations that some people claim to receive now. Our Father is a God of love and mercy and will not withhold any good thing from them that walk uprightly; Psalm 84:11. Many of our mothers and fathers walked uprightly, received all that was good and went to heaven, yet they never dreamed of the "Power" and miraculous demonstrations that some are making such noise about now. We should want to go to heaven and unless we prepare ourselves for heaven, we will not get there. God commands us to prepare, Amos 4:12. What are we to do in making the preparation?

We need to get in possession of the Spirit of Jesus Christ. How? Become Sons of God, Galatians 4:6. In other words what shall we do to become Christian, or to be saved? Let us take the Bible way for it. The question is not what we must do to become a Campbellite; a Methodist; a Baptist; a Presbyterian, but what must we do to become simply a Christian. God wants us to be Christians and nothing more. To the word. Unity

- Believe on Christ John 3:16. God so loved the world that he gave his only begotten Son that whosoever believeth on him shall have everlasting life, Acts, 10:43. To him gave all the prophets witness that through his name, whosoever believeth in him shall receive remission of sins, Acts 16:31. Believe on the Lord Jesus Christ and thou shalt be saved.
- Repent — turn from sin. Luke 24:47. Repentance should be preached in his name, Acts 2:38. Repent, Acts 3:19. Repent, Acts 17:30. God commands all men to repent.
- Confess Christ, Matthew 10:32. Whosoever therefore shall confess me before men, him will I confess before my Father, Acts. 8:37. And he answered and said I believe that Jesus Christ is the Son of God. Romans 10:9 Confess with thy mouth the Lord Jesus.
- Be Baptized, Mark 16:16. He that believeth and is baptized shall be saved. Acts 2:38. Repent and be baptized for the remission of sins. Acts 22:16. Arise and be baptized.
- Do all sincerely calling on the name of the lord, Acts 22;16. Romans 10:13.
- Lead a faithful life, 2 Peter 1:5-11. Add to your faith virtue knowledge, and to knowledge temperance, and to temperance patience, and to patience godliness, and to godliness brotherly kindness, and to brotherly kindness charity — for if ye do

these things, ye shall never fall, 1 Thessalonians 5:15-23. Rejoice evermore. Pray without ceasing. In everything give thanks, for this is the will of God of Christ Jesus concerning you. Quench not the spirit. Despise not prophesyings. Prove all things hold fast that which is good. Abstain from all appearance of evil. And the very God of peace sanctify you wholly; and I pray God your whole spirit, and soul, and body be preserved blameless unto the coming of our Lord Jesus Christ.

The foregoing passages of Scripture reveal to us the gospel plan of salvation from start to finish; and it was devised by divine wisdom. It needs no changing, no addition, no revision. It is perfect and complete, and it demonstrates not only the mercy of God, but also his anxiety to save the world. Let us accept it unreservedly, and give every hour of life to that which is noblest, purest, truest, and best and if disappointment and confusion overtake us in life's journey, we will find heart rest in God. May the word of the Lord which has been sounding for many Ages find ready acceptance in the hearts of all men everywhere. For in the word of God is centered the world's hope, and by it every man is to be made free from all fetters that bind. Let us hope that the hearts of all men may turn toward each other for unity and brotherly love. We long for the tumult of religious wars to be hushed and its dark cloud to dissolve into everlasting nothingness. May selfishness between all God's people perish. We are sure that some of you will join us constantly in the prayer that God may be in the councils of men; that he may have compassion upon all the world according to promise that Jews and Jentiles may be gathered in and then the world may see the rich salvation assured in Jesus Christ, the Lord of Glory.

APPENDIX B

A Summary of 16 Years
J.W. Masters devoted to working with
The State Board of Missions of
The Kentucky Christian Missionary
Convention

Number of Days J.W. Masters spent in the Field during the years 1908 through 1923	He averaged 262 days per year during 1908—911, 1913—1917, and 1919—1921.	In 1912, the number was 356 days. In 1918, the number was 320 days	In 1922/1923, his evangelism efforts were significantly reduced.
Sermons Preached	Total 3,177: Two highest years, 1912 — 356; and 1918 — 320		
Baptisms	Total 850: Two highest years, 1909 — 96; and 1911 — 110		
Members "Reclaimed"	Total 413: Two highest years, 1911 — 83; and 1920 — 63		
Additions by Letter or Statement	Total 714: Two highest years, 1912 — 120; and 1913 — 143		
Additions by other sources	Total 326: Two highest years, 1910 — 56; and 1913 — 37		
Churches served	Total 324: Two highest years, 1911 — 33; and 1912 — 40		

Bible Schools organized	Total 28: 4 Bible Schools organized in each of 3 different years
Prayer meetings organized	Total 8: No year was significantly higher than any other
Churches organized[51]	Total 12: 3 congregations were organized in 1913

---

[51] The list of churches J.W. Masters organized is found in Appendix C.

Appendix C

A List of Churches Established by J.W. Masters

From various sources I have tried to compile an accurate list of the churches organized by J.W. Masters. When available, the dates are included. It is possible Masterstown Christian Church and Masters Chapel Christian Church are the same. It was never stated exactly that he established the Masterstown church or the South Corbin church.

With the inclusion of either of the two above mentioned churches — Masters Chapel or South Corbin — I am able to account for all nineteen (the figure most often mentioned) churches attributed to J.W. Masters by H.W. Elliott.

Then there is another possible scenario. In his funeral remarks, G.E. Chandler said Masters "started the church at Barbourville." In the Corbin Daily Tribune, the editorial comments at the time of Masters' monument dedication say both the Artemus and the Barbourville churches were established by Masters. John Masters could only be given credit for starting the Barbourville church if he indeed, re-established or re-organized it. The reason is obvious, Masters' first regular preaching in Kentucky was in the church in Barbourville when he came from Virginia in 1885. There is no indication the congregation had not been established at that time. Thus, my list omits the Barbourville church and includes three churches in Corbin — First Christian, Masterstown and

Masters Chapel. It is also possible, however, there were others he organized which are not on this list.

As the Corbin Daily Tribune also said in the editorial on the occasion of the monument dedication, the churches on this list constitute "at least 19 churches" organized by J.W. Masters.

Artemus, Knox County, Kentucky	Possibly 1885-88
Pineville, Bell County	1886
Rose Hill, Virginia	Possibly 1887-1888
Richlands Christian Church, Knox County	Probably 1887
Corbin, First Christian	1892
Rogersville, Tennessee	1898
Shepherdsville, Kentucky	1898
Jellico, Tennessee	1899
Corbin, Masterstown Christian	Probably 1901-1902
Corbin, Masters Chapel	
Puckett's Creek, Bell County	1907
Harlan, Harlan Christian	1908
Hyden, Leslie County	1909
Cranks Creeks, Harlan County	1912
Happy Valley	
Brodhead, Rockcastle County	Probably 1916
Manchester, Clay County (reorganization)	1917
Fogertown, Clay County	1918
Gum Sulphur, Rockcastle County	Probably 1920

APPENDIX D

Funeral Message by G. E. Chandler "A Tribute to a Pioneer" ("A Tribute to a Pioneer" Christian Standard, November 15, 1924)

We have met today to pay a last sad tribute to the great man whose body rests for a moment here in our midst. The scripture is full of wonderful texts, any of which might serve as a basis for a message of comfort to these sorrowing dear ones. "Precious in the sight of God is the death of his saints." "Blessed are the dead who die in the Lord from henceforth," etc. Any of these great texts would be wonderfully fitting. But I search further. A text that speaks more of life than of death claims my attention. "Let us make man!" These words were spoken by the Lord when the earth was ready for the first pioneer. They mean far more than the making of a physical body. From that day to this God has been making man. The Bible is the record of the great undertaking, and life furnishes some fine examples of the finished product.

When God made John Wesley Masters, he made a man.

1. He was a man in life achievement. Born in 1854, he spent his boyhood in the troublous days of civil strife... Like many another of the pioneers, he got his education at home by the light of the pine knot. Few years of schooling figured in his young life, and yet a college graduate might have envied his English, and

have been pleased to sit at his feet and learn the truths of the old book. At the age of 10 he decided to be a Dunkard preacher, like his father. But he read his Bible with such discernment that he was soon questioning his father about the church of the Book, and with such effect as to turn him from the Dunkard ministry to the plain church of Christ, to which ministry he himself naturally turned.

The story of his early life reveals some striking characteristics. Determination, courage, conviction stand out boldly. Hopelessly handicapped with a stutterer's tongue, he set out to overcome it. People pitied him, and made fun of his efforts, but he wrought so well that he finally became fluent of speech, and was the welcome preacher at every Christian Church in the hills, whether large or small.

He faced every challenge of life fearlessly. The rugged hills called, and he went, threading his way alone along many an unkept track in the dead of night. Nature in her angriest moods sent floods and storms, and still he went; he never missed an appointment; he never turned back. Man took a hand in trying to deter him: schoolhouses were locked; opponents challenged; he met them fearlessly in debate, "contending for the faith once delivered unto the saints," and he won. No obstacle could hold this man; he went courageously on.

Deep conviction held him true to his trust. He saw the need, counted the cost and made the sacrifice. Tempted when the larder was empty and the meal in the barrel was low, he turned for a time to the study of law, and again, to medicine, but to no purpose. True as the needle of the compass, he swung back to his life's purpose. In later years a friend reproved him, saying, "you might have been rich now if you had finished law." He answered, "I will have all the riches I need at the judgment." This man lived to noble purpose, and achieved a great life's work. Thousands rejoice today because J.W. Masters triumphed over difficulties, and blazed a trail through these hills.

2. He was a man in his dealings with his follow man. He was upright in every transaction. His word was his bond. Some may have disagreed with him, but all respected and loved him.

Men who opposed him on the platform of debate claimed him as a friend. A certain preacher, with whom he had two debates, stood up at the close of the last of these and said, "There is not a preacher in my own faith who has a warmer place in my heart than Brothers Masters."

He was benevolent and charitable.

"Careless their merits or their faults to scan,
He pity gave ere charity began."

He spent his life as one who served. He loved to entertain his friends, and would sit by the hour, in his later days, telling the incidents of his younger life, with a quiet humor that was refreshing. My first visit to his home was a hurried one. I went to see the man who was so universally loved, to confer with him about the work in these hills. After a delightful talk I mentioned that I had but a short time before my train was due. But he would not hear of me leaving without a meal in his home. It was the nearest I ever came to offending him. I must remain. Dinner was rapidly prepared, and rapidly eaten, and after a long hard run, I barely caught the train. Standing here today, I am glad I took that meal, for it showed me the heart of the man "who lived in a house by the side of the road," and who was showing to the world the spirit of hospitality of a bygone day.

3. He was a man in dignity and poise. Always serene and steady, he was the master of every situation. He never lost his grip. He was a calming influence in the sick-room, a comforter in the chamber of death. He was eagerly sought for to grace a wedding-feast, and was brought for miles to stand as a defender of the faith. Living in a day of debates, he became a great debater, snatching victory out of seeming defeat. He knew when to speak and when to hold a dignified silence. Though often urged by his brethren to retreat in the face of overwhelming opposition, he went right on preaching the Word, contending for the faith, doing the work of an evangelist, reproving, rebuking, exhorting, calming, strengthening, establishing; and through it all he was master, poised and steady. Goldsmith's lines wonderfully fit this noble life.

"As some tall cliff that lifts its awful form,
Swells from the vale and midway leaves the storm,
Though round its breast the rolling clouds are spread,
Eternal sunshine settles on its head."

4. He was a man in service of God and humanity. Like the prophet of old, he heard the call, and answered, "'Here am I; send me.'" He stands among the noble band of men called pioneers. His type is far too rare today. Men who, for the love of their fellow-man, would preach the gospel to the regions beyond; who have learned in whatsoever state they find themselves therewith to be content. This noble man, J.W. Masters, after leading his father to the truth, was baptized, and, in turn, baptized all of his brothers and sisters, and then set out on horseback to find others. On four occasions, to use his own language, he preached himself afoot; that is, he had to sell his horse to pay his store account. For a ten days' meeting he was paid a quarter. Once he was offered a farm, if he would turn to another faith. He answered, "I would not leave the church of Jesus Christ to stay overnight with any other." He sought advancement only where truth would advance. Like Moses, he chose to suffer. It seems incredible that he was able to carry on, "but he endured as seeing one who is invisible." Later the way became brighter. The Kentucky State Board employed him as an evangelist to the hills. How many converts he made, or how many churches he established, will never be known here, but, during the 22 years he was with the State Board, he added 3,270 to the church. Practically every church in these hills was established by his efforts. Harlan, Pineville, Barbourville, Corbin and Jellico grace the long list.

He died in the harness, having just returned from a meeting the day before his death. His call was swift and sudden. Perhaps, if he could have given a message before he went, words like those of Moody would have fallen from his lips. "Earth is receding; heaven is opening; God is calling me." A great man has fallen. I would rather have the record of John W. Masters, and have accomplished what he has for the kingdom of God in these hills, than be the governor of a state or the President of the United States. He was a great preacher, a loving husband, an affectionate father and a firm friend.

APPENDIX E

A Tribute to J.W. Masters by J. C. Eagle (The Corbin Daily Tribune October 4, 1950)

Mr. Chairman, ladies, gentlemen and relatives of J.W. Masters, deceased. We are met here again to pay tribute and memory to a great pioneer mountain evangelist.

This is not a funeral. It is a day of joy, gladness and memory. If J.W. Masters could look down from heaven on this little band, I fancy I could hear him quoting some of the sayings of the Master, as he spoke to His little band of aggrieved disciples. "Let not your heart be troubled, ye believe in God, believe in me. In my Father's house are many mansions, if it were not so, I would have told you; I go to prepare a place for you. I will come again and receive you unto myself, that where I am, there ye may be also."

While the memory of our friends and loved ones linger in our minds for months and years, we too often neglect to have a home gathering in which to refresh our memory of them. The greatest monument erected to anyone is not an epitaph on stacks of marble and granite; but is a lasting memory lingering in the hearts and minds of loved ones.

So, on this occasion, I count it a real joy to try to speak a few words in memory and honor of a great friend and hero who so untiringly disseminated the New Testament faith over mountains, hill and dale.

My first sight of J.W. Masters was 55 years ago. He preached in our immediate neighborhood on "What Must I Do To Be Saved?" We were all Methodists. I had never heard anything like it. It was scriptural, logical and convincing. Little did I think then of our near future companionship for he became one of my dearest friends and benefactors. A little later he baptized me, my wife, and later my present wife; several years later he baptized my aged mother.

When Gilbert E. Chandler preached J.W. Masters' funeral on Oct. 5, 1924, he by-passed some desirable texts such as: "Precious in the sight of the Lord are the deaths of His Saints" "Blessed are the dead who die in the Lord — for their works do follow them" and some of Paul's last words: "I have fought the good fight, I have finished the course, I have kept the faith. Henceforth there is the crown of life laid up for me, and not for me only, but for all who love His appearing."

Any one of these texts would have been very fitting to have given comfort and cheer to those bereft, but Rev. Chandler chose one which speaks more of life: "Let us make man."

Brother Chandler stated,

"When God made John Wesley Masters, He made a man, every inch a man, a man of life achievement."

Born in 1854, Rev. Masters spent his boyhood days in the Civil strife. Like many other pioneers, he got his education at home by the light of the pine knot. Few years of schooling figured in his young life, and yet, a college graduate might have envied his English. "The heights of great men reached and kept, were not attained by sudden flight, but they while their companions slept, were toiling upward in the night."

The great lecturer, W.J. Bryan, pictured a wonderful thought when he said: "Each nation is in a large measure responsible to the oncoming generations to hand down to posterity the finer and better things of life."

Personally, I have a sort of hobby, of trying to ascertain what our ancestors have accomplished that is worthy of handing down to posterity. Briefly, we realize that the discoverers, the settlers, the heroes of war did accomplish much; the inventors, the scientists and doctors have played a great part, but when it comes down to the mountain evangelist who went through some of Paul's perils in bringing souls to Christ, is not this "the greater works ye shall do" that the Master speaks of in John 14:12?

Having a great intellectual ability, a clear, keen, logical mind, a great reader and close student of the word of God, Rev. Masters early became known as a strong defender of the faith. He accumulated a large library of good books authorized by the ablest preachers, who stood firmly for the restoration movement of New Testament Christianity. He forged his way into the apostolic church, taught his household the way more perfectly, and baptized them including his saintly father and mother.

His day was a day of debates and he was a champion in the game. He never challenged, but was ready to accept any challenge, strongly contending for the faith once for all delivered to the saints. He knew no compromise. He knew the word and had the nerve to proclaim it. He never altered the meaning of the scriptures to please his hearers for money or additions. He, like Paul, shrank not from declaring the whole council of God.

He was an ardent prohibitionist and fighter of sin. He died in the harness, having returned from a revival only the day before. He was a man who lived by the side of the road and was a friend to man.

APPENDIX F

A Tribute and Poems to J.W. Masters
by Thomas Taylor
The Long Trail or Circuit of One Mountain
Minister ("The Long Trail or Circuit of one
Mountain Minister," Renfro Revelations, A
Magazette Williamsburg, Kentucky, Volume
8, Number 3, March, 1951)

I was invited to make a historic talk, on September 17, at the Homecoming Service in memory of the life and work of Rev. John W. Masters. I long ago had taught school at Masterstown, and was very glad to be present. My sketch that I wrote for this special occasion is as follows. THOMAS TAYLOR

Rev. John Masters was one individual of one of the romantic group of characters that became famous in American literature through the pens of some of America's leading authors of fiction of the colorful period known as the gay 90's, and also of the days of the early part of the twentieth century: those hardy, tireless characters spoken of sometimes as Circuit Riders. Those who have read John Fox, Jr's. novel, will remember the sentence in the story of the death of Lonesome, when there were no services sung or spoken, because the circuit rider was then miles away — a clear picture of the life of a preacher who rode far across the hills to speak at the little churches or chapels of the mountaineers, as the people of those out-of-the-way places had come to be known; and some of our greatest men of affairs were of this branch of the religious-minded settlers of our highland regions, as was President Woodrow Wilson, who once said with seeming pride: "My own ancestors were Scotch Highlanders." It was on the long, dismal circuits leading to these scattered groups of Christians that Brother Masters did most of his fifty years in the Christian ministry. He always seemed anxious and willing to serve these who found it hard to secure pastors.

Yes, Brother Masters often preached to some of the State's best churches; he was at one time pastor of the church at Glasgow; and was founder of the church at Corbin. I recall the first time I ever saw him. I was a small boy then. It was early in the 1890's at Woodbine, where a prosperous new church had been organized by some of the Mountain-region's best people, who had in some instances come from other sections of the State, to enter business in the new town which was then [the] nearest railroad station to many points like Middlesboro, that was being built then by English engineers, backed by a London, England bank.

I can still recall the attention and respect shown the minister on that fine Sunday morning, when many came with the beautiful flowers that had somehow through some now-unknown source given Woodbine its new name to take the place of Joefields that was once used to honor the place's historic first settler, Joseph Johnson. Rev. John Masters was a speaker of fine appearance, and a gifted speaker, with an unusual store of knowledge of the Bible and things pertaining to religion and the Church. I attended his debates with the Rev. William Estes that were of interest to a vast audience of hearers.

William Estes was one of Rev. Masters' principal rivals in this section. He also was a brilliant public speaker; and once I heard him classed as one of Whitley County's leading orators —

I myself would say that Masters was a greater debater than Estes. Yet he was of a different personality. I suppose for many it might have been hard to decide which was the most winning speaker. Rev. Masters was of the more modern type, more like the average radio speaker of the present day — was more humorous.

It is not always those who seek most to be honored that find places in the halls of memory, though these may sometimes be written up for pay in some cheap publication. John Masters did not seem to care for praise or publicity. Yet, we feel sure that he would, if he could look back today, be pleased to see that the long trail, extending fifty years and which took the best part of his useful life, is remembered by his friends and all who have seen, at one time or another, some of the harvest — the golden harvest — of the fields in which he toiled; some of the sheaves of the seeds he had sown.

John Masters was founder of the Christian College at Corbin, early in the history of the town. For a time it was under the head of Prof. F.C. Buttons who later on became one of the State's educational leaders, and filled an important position at Frankfort under Prof. T.J. Coates, forty years ago. Among the prominent friends of Bro. Masters were Congressmen Vincent Boreing and D.T. Chestnut, who was one of the pioneer business men of Corbin, one of the first church leaders, and founder of Corbin's first newspaper, The Corbin Enterprise.

> He never seemed to care for wealth,
> He never sought for fame—
> He seemed content to find his place,
> Led in the Master's name,
> Where usefulness was rift and where
> The fields of harvest lay
> Awaiting workers with the faith
> To strive from day to day.
> He seemed to ever look ahead
> T'ward some ungarnered yield
> That seemed at harvest-time to call
> On a neglected field.

On his desk he kept his Bible,
In his heart its echoes clear
Forever sounded thru the minutes
And he knew no sense of fear.
Often on the edge of shadows —
With the world again at war —
He was calmed to find that Spirit
From the pens of days afar,
When in Galilee, and Sardis
First the Words became a flame.
Guiding little bands of Christians
Who had learned a name — a name.

TO THE MEMORY OF J.W. MASTERS
This to the memory of the work he did
To bring these mountains the gifts of truth
That had guided Paul and James and John —
The blessings of Eternal Youth.
This to the memory of those older days
When he came to Corbin to here begin
His work, that religion, also held
Light to in the fields of learning win.
This to the memory of the fight he made
On superstitions that had reigned too long,
Handed down from forebears — good
In meaning, with myths that were often wrong.
This to the memory of the work he left
To last till Judgment and the end of time:
Each year the setting of a golden stage
Where his role was played grows more sublime.

Thos Taylor, Sept. 20, 58

Appendix G

A Tribute to J.W. Masters
by The Editor of The Christian Standard
"Men Called Pioneers" ("Men Called
Pioneers" Christian Standard,
November 15, 1924)

Our columns this week are given a solemn dignity by the appearance of the funeral oration delivered by Gilbert E. Chandler over the grave of John W. Masters at Corbin, Ky. It is the passing of a veteran in the faith, and a reverential tribute from one who knows the value of the principles to whose advancement J.W. Masters gave the full measure of his devotion.

We cannot stay the melancholy which smites upon our heart as the thin line vanishes — the thin fair line of the fathers who sowed our furrows, who fought the good fight, and who finish their course with the faith unsurrendered and uncorrupted.

It is the contrast which is heart-breaking. As the venerable pioneers, full of faith and good fruits, pass on, there appears an empty-handed army of timeservers to take their place, battalions of soft sentimentalists and self-seekers, rank and file of well-clad figures strutting about and gossiping over old wives' fables.

This old evangelist of the Kentucky hills was not college bred, and yet, as his eulogist says, a college graduate might have envied his English and his knowledge of the Bible. Today the college graduate gets everything else but education in his mother tongue and the work of God, and these accomplishments are the center and circumference of a preacher's power.

He faced hardship without complaints "threading his way alone along many an unkept track" to carry the Word of life to the destitute hill country. Sectarian opposition never deterred him. He met the denominationalists in their own stronghold, and vanquished them with the sword of the Spirit. The prophets today, who enter into the labors of these great hearts, too often prefer to wear soft raiment, and speak smooth prophecies which please the people, and are inoffensive to "our sister churches."

"His word was his bond. All respected him." Such were the Pioneers. The breed of Jesuits had not then entered in, to break the morale and power of a movement whose passion was truth. Disingenuous is a word unknown then, but now needed for a race whose movements are planned and carried out in the shadow zone.

Chandler says of him: "Practically every church of note in these hills was established by his efforts — Harlan, Pineville, Barbourville, Corbin and Jellico gracing the list." In many regions today the Don Quixotes help the churches die which the pioneers founded and left flourishing. Deaf ears are turned to the waste places which wait for the gospel, while eager feet hasten to the call of comfort and ease.

The times do not brand heroes, because the times are out of joint. Why expect Restoration trailblazers when we have "brotherhood agencies" to do the work?

We'll soon wake up, let us hope, to the fact that dollars are mighty poor substitutes for pioneers.

There is a star of hope on the horizon. Read our new columns from week to week, and you will find evidence of a new birth of the old faith, a revival of the Restoration. Here and there over the land we see a new line of heroes rising from the dead level of denominational politics, a series of gospel preachers worthy to wear the ermine which has fallen unstained from the shoulders of the men called pioneers.

APPENDIX H

The First Christian Church Celebrates its Forty-Fifth Anniversary August 8, 1942 Corbin, Kentucky

On August 8, 1942 the First Christian Church of Corbin, Kentucky, of which F.N. Wolfe is minister, held a meeting in celebration of its forty-fifth anniversary.

Forty-five years ago, when the city of Corbin was little more than a village, John Masters, with the assistance of other loyal workers, organized and established here what is today one of the leading Christian Churches of the state.

Previous to this, there had been bodies of Christians at Woodbine and other nearby places, some of whom had just moved into Corbin, which promised to become a thriving railroad center. At first there was a very modest frame building; and for a time the Christian College, also founded by Brother Masters, was used for worship. Today the church has one of the best structures in the states.

The long, eventful trail of the minister, whose career in the mountain regions of Virginia and Kentucky is the subject of this article, began in Virginia — almost, if not actually, in sight of the famous Trail of the Lonesome Pine. Some of the long church houses and schools at which he preached, as well as many of the homes of the early members of his church, and the customs and speech of those members themselves were much like those in the setting of Mr. Fox books. That minister's rustic trail passed out of Virginia through historic Cumberland Gap, and on up the valleys to the heads of the woodland streams, some of which also are well known through the writing of John Fox, novelist. In riding over this trail to preach back in the 70's, Brother Masters was what some in that region called a "circuit rider."

In fact, the region, which the minister often referred to as "Beyond the Gap," was what a college professor many years later called in his book, "the land of the saddlebags," from the old custom of riding over the hills on horseback with the well known saddlebags used by mountaineers for carrying everything from moonshine liquor and guns to groceries, articles of clothing and hymn books, stationery and Bibles. Brother Masters, who was born in Virginia in 1854, was the son of a very successful Dunkard preacher; so the boy, at an early age, decided to be a minister also. At first he thought only of being a Dunkard preacher; but when he began to read to prepare himself to speak and took note that the Bible never mentioned the Dunkard religion, but spoke only of the Christians, which name he learned had once been applied at Antioch, he gave up the idea of representing anything but the church that was established in the early days of the era by Christ Himself. The hard struggle of a mountain boy of that time to prepare for a career of any kind may be understood from the statement that Brother Masters went to work at ten cents per day to secure money to educate himself for the Christian ministry. He worked at this rate for some time, until a friend influenced him to turn to the study at law as a more profitable career. Scarcely had he begun the study of law — which was never his own voluntary selection as a profession — when he returned to his home in Virginia (for that was in Magoffin County, Kentucky) and began to preach. This was in 1874. During the days of that first attempt at preaching, he studied the Bible in an impartial way, and read the sermons of Benjamin Franklin, and made desperate efforts to cure himself of the habit of stammering. Once he swallowed a rifle ball, and, another time, let one drop from his mouth, in his attempt, which he often told of in his humorous moods. But at last he completely overcame the defect, and soon began to win fame as a debater.

As a debater, he was a speaker of striking personality of speech. Though a product of the hills, his dress was never the quaint type so frequently described by writers as belonging to mountain clergy. He dressed as well as the Congressman from his district, and at least one Congressman from Kentucky was one of his personal friends. In debate he quoted from the Bible and from works of well-known writers, used wit and satire, and stuck to logic and philosophy.

There came years of hard times and little pay. Often riding for miles, through deep snow late at night, over hills, on horseback to reach the little churches far up at the heads of the creeks, delivering his sermons and returning home with only a few cents as payment for his pains, he finally experienced the worries that had beset so many before him, and which are still a part of preaching the truth with many ministers. So, after many plans and heartaches and halting between opinions, he decided to give up, in part, at least, debating and preaching, and to take up the study of medicine.

The outlook in the field of medicine began to grow dim before him, so he sold his medicine books, etc., and decided to return to the study of law, but soon was convinced he should return to preaching — this time for good. He went to work with greater zeal and plans to combat every opposition, remembering the experiences of Paul, who had fought with the beast in the arena of Ephesus. He gained courage — and friends — and secured great additions to the church. The question of his life work was settled.

During the long career of this minister, he rode many thousands of miles on horseback to preach, his journeys taking him often up to the heads of many streams. He often told of preaching on Hell for Sartin, the place that furnished John Fox, Jr., with the material, as well as the name, for his first published story. Other creeks where he debated and preached were Bob's Creek, Wallin's Creek, Bowen's Creek, Puckett's Creek, Bullskin

Creek, Meadow Creek, Indian Creek and Goose Creek. Once or more he held meetings under cliffs. One of these, on Laurel River, near Corbin, known as Meetinghouse Rock, continued for many years after the coming of the railroads to be used as a place of worship by the church which Brother Masters founded in that section. He often preached under the trees and sometimes at the homes of members of the church. Log schoolhouses also were used.

In one of his best-known books, John Fox wrote: "There was no service sung or spoken over the dead, for the circuit rider was then months away." Brother Masters preached hundreds of those funerals months after the date of death. It was a common custom in the hills in those days, because ministers were few and their "circuits" often long and rough, with the saddle horse the fastest means of travel.

While the nearest railroad point was still fifty miles from the churches he served, the minister made a trip, half the way on horseback, to Lexington, where he met J.W. McGarvey, who from that date on had a far-reaching influence over his life and work, for McGarvey was at that time one among the leading authorities on the doctrines of the church in the South.

Brother Masters soon began to organize Christian Churches in the small towns, and he accepted the ministry of the church at Glasgow, which he held for some time. He also served for a time as pastor at London.

Among his admiring friends who were substantial aids to him during the most trying days of his career were some of the most prominent men of that section of the state. One of these was the Congressman of the famous Eleventh District, Honorable Vincent Boreing; another, Judge Moss of Pineville; another, one of the founders of Corbin, D.T. Chestnut, an influential politician and editor. Mr. Chestnut never forgot the financial needs of the church.

Even after he became busy with the work of churches in the towns and villages, Brother Masters continued to ride long trips to little churches far up the creeks or over the hills. On these trips he frequently discussed the all-important topic to someone that he chanced to meet along these trails. One farmer to whom he thus spoke termed the advice given, "A Sermon in the Saddle," and, if we could but know, these short sermons alone may have had surprising effects.

(The original printed program for the 45th Anniversary celebration of the Corbin congregation also included information relative to another personality in Eastern Kentucky. Since it has no relationship in any way to Mr. Masters, that material is not included here in this printing.)

Appendix I

Newspaper Article Regarding
Monument Dedication of Pioneer Minister
("Rev. Lester D. Palmer to Dedicate
Monument at Grave of Pioneer Minister,
Masters," The Corbin Daily Tribune,
September 22, 1958)

The Rev. Lester Palmer, Lexington, associational general secretary of the Christian Churches of Kentucky, will speak at First Christian Church in Corbin Sunday morning and will deliver the dedicatory address at the unveiling of a monument at the grave of the Rev. J.W. Masters in Pine Hill Cemetery in the afternoon.

The morning service will be at 10:45 o'clock at the church.

The afternoon dedication service will be at 2:00 p.m. EST at the graveside, if weather permits.

If the weather is unsuitable for an outside service, the rite will be held in the First Christian Church, First and Kentucky Avenue in Corbin.

The Rev. Masters came to Kentucky in 1885 as a minister and evangelist. He was instrumental in establishing at least 19 churches among them two at Corbin, one at Bush in Laurel County and those at Artemus, Barbourville, and Pineville. At least 3,270 persons came into these and other churches of the brotherhood under his ministry and evangelism, which lasted nearly a half-century.

The monument project was sponsored by the Ministerial Association of Christian Churches, made up of ministers and lay members of the counties of Knox, Laurel and Whitley. The marker was purchased by donations from individuals and churches in Southeast Kentucky and adjacent areas.

William Whitaker, layman of the First Christian Church, London, and president of the Ministerial Association will preside. The opening prayer will be offered by Rev. Ashley Garland, pastor of the Whetstone Christian Church. This will be followed by a song, "In the Sweet By and By," by the choir of the First Christian Church, Corbin.

The Rev. William M. Huie, pastor of the Corbin church, will then speak on "Brother J.W. Masters, His Life and Work," after which he will introduce members of the Masters family. Then will follow the dedication address by the Rev. Palmer.[52]

The Rev. S.H. Masters, son of the pioneer preacher, will unveil the monument, assisted by the Rev. Marion Parkey and the Rev. David Blondell, grandson and great grandson respectively. The choir will sing "Faith of Our Fathers," after which benediction will be pronounced by the Rev. Grant Reed, pastor of the Lily Christian Church.

---

[52] In checking three sources, I was unsuccessful in obtaining a copy of the remarks of either Bill Huie or Lester Palmer for that occasion. Although the material either one would have used was regarding the same source — J.W. Masters. Nonetheless, the uniqueness of style of each writer would have been interesting to have seen. Dr. Palmer told me that he presumed that the Kentucky Regional Office had kept a copy of his remarks. But neither the Regional Office nor the Disciples of Christ Historical Society could locate this material.

BIOGRAPHY

David N. Blondell is a native of Middlesboro, Ky., and is a retired minister of the Christian Church (Disciples of Christ). Beginning as a student pastor and then in full time ministry, his pastorates were in Virginia, Alabama and principally Kentucky.

His ministerial concentration has been in the local church. Through forty years of ministry, he focused on church growth through preaching and evangelism, and broadening the church's mission focus through World Outreach. He served the wider church through denominational and ecumenical interests. While serving congregations, he conducted numerous evangelism workshops in Virginia and Kentucky, and preached dozens of revival meetings in Alabama and Kentucky.

Formal education includes the Bachelor of Arts degree from Johnson Bible College; Master of Divinity and Doctor of Ministry degrees both from Lexington Theological Seminary.

Father of three and grandfather of four, he and his wife Julia have lived in Lexington, Ky. for the past 41 years, where he was Senior Minister of Crestwood Christian Church for 26 years. He retired from the pastorate in 1994.